WAREHOUSE HOME

WAREHOUSE HOME

INDUSTRIAL INSPIRATION FOR TWENTY-FIRST-CENTURY LIVING

Sophie Bush

with 375 illustrations

Thames & Hudson

CONTENTS

Opposite left:
Loft 19 by A+Z design studio
Photographed by Beppe Brancato
Opposite right:
Upholstery Factory by
Mark Lewis Interior Design
Photographed by Rory Gardiner

CASE STUDY KEY

Design Insights
From The Architect

Personal Perspectives
From The Homeowner

INTRODUCTION

Four years ago, my husband and I bought our home in a Grade II-listed warehouse conversion in south-east London. I still remember the first time we caught sight of the enormous Victorian granary on the bank of the River Thames. The sheer scale of it was so impressive. A dormant crane, retired from service, bowed its head over the water and, far above, the rooftop water towers kept watch across the city skyline. Throughout the conversion we found fascinating remnants of a previous life. The building continues to have an effect on me, even now. And I owe it a great deal, because it has not only been our home, it also inspired me to launch *Warehouse Home* – an independent publication that has now been enjoyed in over sixty countries worldwide.

In this first *Warehouse Home* book, we travel from New York to Melbourne, London to Hong Kong, visiting some of the most inspirational industrial conversions in the world. We have made an important distinction between industrial and 'industrial style', reviewing only those homes in conversions with a genuine industrial or manufacturing past. From live–work spaces to family-friendly lofts, substantial developments to single-family dwellings, we showcase remarkable residences in historic granaries, former textile factories, tanneries, old printworks and, of course, warehouses. And we celebrate the original architectural features that make these homes truly unique: exposed timber beams and bare brickwork, structural columns and industrial doors.

Most of us share a sense of fascination and pride in our respective nations' rich industrial histories, reflected in these heritage buildings. Our own warehouse narrowly avoided destruction during the intensive bombing raids of World War II. The surrounding timber yards, docks and warehouses were almost entirely destroyed. During the post-war era, the decline of several industries and the modernization of others further threatened the future of the factories and warehouses that were once at the very heart of a global industrial revolution. For many years, decommissioned tanneries and tobacco factories, former pumping stations and printworks in cities around the world remained derelict, under the constant threat of demolition. But an exciting potential still remained.

The 'loft living' phenomenon, the transformation of industrial shells for habitation, has its origins in 1950s New York. At this time the middle classes were leaving overcrowded and polluted Manhattan for the family-friendly suburbs. In their wake came artists, attracted by the generous proportions of the derelict industrial buildings, breathing new life into the area known today as SoHo (South of Houston Street). Late nineteenth-century cast-iron-frame former warehouses were available for cut-price rents and were soon repurposed for bohemian and basic, innovative (if often illegal) living accommodation. New York's City Planning Commission had intended to demolish older buildings, like these, to clear a path for a new expressway. But with the arrival of these new, creative inhabitants, SoHo had started to flourish; the economic potential did not go unnoticed and the neighbourhood, and its buildings, were granted a reprieve. Furthermore, a report commissioned in 1963 concluded that the distinctive cast-iron warehouses of

◄■ Grade II-listed New Concordia Wharf is set at the mouth of St Saviour's Dock on the River Thames. It was built in 1885 as a grain warehouse at a time when the surrounding district, known today as Shad Thames, comprised the largest warehouse complex in London. Spices, coffee and other commodities were unloaded directly from river boats.

'A dormant crane, retired from service, bowed its head over the river. Rooftop water towers kept watch across the city skyline. Throughout the conversion we found remnants of a former life.'

the area south of Houston were an integral part of New York's heritage. Laws were amended to foster their redevelopment and young professionals began seeking out these warehouse conversions as much trendier, and far less conventional, condominiums. Residences that had once been avant-garde were now aspirational, and by the 1990s, developers such as the Manhattan Loft Corporation and Urban Splash had transformed several iconic industrial complexes in the USA, UK and abroad. Films such as *Wall Street* (1987) and the sitcom *Friends* (1994–2004) popularized the 'loft living' phenomenon.

Over time, dwindling housing stocks and a growing disillusionment with carbon-copy contemporary homes have made these conversions ever more covetable. They are relatively scarce and excite something of a pioneering spirit: a passionate desire to preserve, protect and improve. Evocative names hint at past purposes and far-flung places: The Hat Factory, Oriental Warehouse, Cinnamon Wharf, Tobacco Dock, The Maltings. Indeed, when the waterfront warehouses in the Shad Thames area of London were converted into homes in the 1990s, the first residents were still able to detect the century-old aromas of the spices they had once stored. These former industrial buildings offer adaptable space and distinctive backdrops for individual expression. Whether cool and cavernous in concrete or brick-built and heavily beamed, these buildings have plenty of grit and character and are an exciting blank canvas for interior design enthusiasts. The normal rules for interior decoration do not apply; architectural and design innovation is possible, indeed more possible here than in any other kind of building.

For architects and designers, these industrial conversions often come with practical and aesthetic considerations that are far removed from those implied by a conventional residence. Often the very fabric of their construction has been left uncovered or untouched: brickwork, cast-iron columns, wooden beams and trusses, and, of course, those distinctive warehouse windows. The creative challenge is how to juxtapose these raw industrial qualities with the requirements and accoutrements of modern-day lifestyles or family living.

Not only are they aspirational, these distinctive, remarkable conversions have also engendered a popular 'industrial chic' aesthetic. Homeowners and interior designers alike around the world are channelling the warehouse look in a variety of creative ways. The second section of our book, therefore, showcases 'Decorative Details', offering insider tips and ideas for achieving a unique warehouse-style feel in any home.

There is a renewed nostalgia for the hallmarks of our nations' industrial heritage; iconic designs that were once produced for the factory floor are now highly sought after. Large quantities of furniture and industrial lighting are being saved from derelict factories; structural timbers and condemned machinery are being salvaged from the scrapheap and imaginatively reused and repurposed.

Four years ago, a warehouse conversion in London became my home and inspired me to launch a global media brand. Whether you live in an industrial building yourself or simply wish to channel the aesthetic, I hope that this debut *Warehouse Home* book inspires you to live, and work, in a new, individual way. *Sophie Bush*

Bright Common architecture and design practice transformed this former pickle factory in the historic Fishtown ➤➤ neighbourhood of Philadelphia into a flexible live–work space for a fine art photographer and his family. The motor fixed to the original, beamed ceiling of the kitchen is from the old service elevator and is an eye-catching feature.

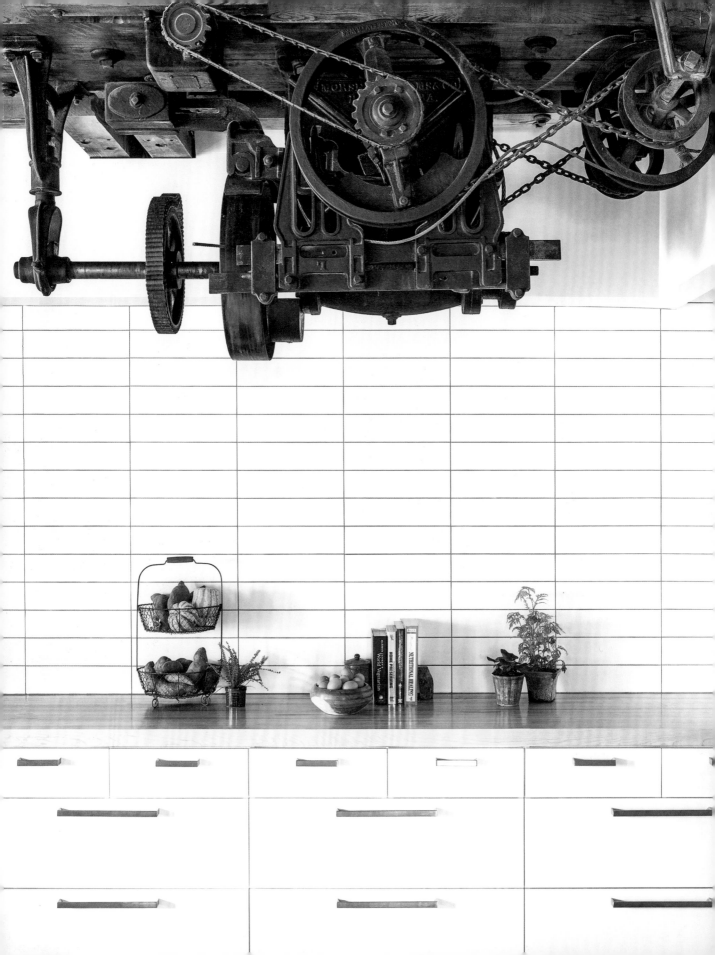

ARCHITECTURAL FEATURES

COLUMNS

A key feature of industrial buildings through the decades has been their open and unobstructed floor plans. The lack of internal walls maximizes light and accommodates as much machinery and as many workers as possible. Load-bearing columns provide essential and space-efficient structural support in these expanses. From sizeable wooden uprights to heavy-duty steel, cast-iron and concrete columns, colonnades and individual columns define most warehouse and factory residences. The scale of the uprights often enhances the dramatic height and character of industrial conversions. Depending on the age and previous purpose of a building, columns may be very plain and the more imposing for their substantial height and girth. Some pillars, however, can be surprisingly decorative as well as sizeable, their designs firmly rooted in the Classical Architectural Orders, developed by the ancient Greeks. Reconfiguring commercial spaces for residential use, architects and homeowners can find original column placement a constraint. But more often, their layout can be cleverly utilized to mark out a living area for a particular function.

◀◀ When LINEOFFICE Architecture undertook the interior renovation of this 111m² (1,200ft²) loft in San Francisco's SoMa neighbourhood, they designed new elements to complement the existing Douglas fir columns and ceilings but kept the scheme simple.

1.

'Built in 1867, San Francisco's Oriental Warehouse was the primary distribution point for the Pacific Mail Steamship Co. and imported tea, rice and silk from Asia. Its original timbers bear marks from that past life.'

ROBERT EDMONDS, EDMONDS + LEE ARCHITECTS

WOODEN

Generally found in much older, pre-twentieth-century warehouses and industrial buildings, timber columns are usually very plain verticals of the same width top and bottom, with very little or no adornment. As wood lacks the strength of metal, timber columns are placed more frequently.

1. Responsible for a loft renovation in the landmark Oriental Warehouse, San Francisco, Edmonds + Lee Architects contrasted original timber with sleek finishes.

2. Alloy architects converted a former New York Brillo warehouse into eight substantial lofts with 4m-high (13ft) ceilings. Towering columns define the lofts' characters.

3.

3. This former distribution warehouse in San Francisco was originally built in 1916. It was transformed into a minimalist loft by Garcia Tamjidi Architecture Design and has the appearance (and calm) of a live-in gallery. The use of brilliant white and clear glass distinguishes new interventions from the original features, particularly the Douglas fir columns and beams. The crisp white surfaces also enhance the sense of spaciousness created by the double-height ceiling and open-plan scheme. A staircase leads from the gallery-inspired living space below to the private residence on the upper level. A glass 'diving board' above the kitchen is a vantage point from which to enjoy the artworks on display. Select furniture, lighting and decorative accessories all adhere to the monochromatic scheme. Oversized black-and-white fine art photographs by Gottfried Helnwein balance the towering timber columns nearby.

CONCRETE

Concrete pillars and columns add a distinctly industrial impression to any interior space and are often more substantial than other types. A rough finish might be complemented by the use of different tactile furnishings and decorative accessories. Smooth or polished concrete columns can be utilized to create a more industrial luxe-style home.

4. In this 1920s factory conversion in downtown San Antonio, Texas, Poteet Architects used an original concrete column in the bathroom as the crowning structure above his-and-hers showers.

5. Painting every concrete surface, including the columns, in a brilliant white gave the loft a bright, modern look, ideal for its art collector owners. The finish draws out the industrial textures.

6.

METAL

From steel and aluminium I-beams to older, cast-iron columns, metal uprights immediately amplify the industrial character of an old factory or warehouse conversion. Black and grey are the traditional finishes.

6. The original features of this 309m² (3,329ft²) loft in a former factory in Cape Town's Woodstock suburb have been very sensitively preserved. A box room inserted between the old metal columns houses a bathroom/dressing room behind full-height library shelves.

7. The apartment is decorated with colourful bric-a-brac and vintage pieces sourced by the owner. A heavily patinated Joko Tea advertisement, affixed to the central island, adds a splash of orange in the open-plan kitchen and offsets black metal columns.

8.

9.

ORNATE

The juxtaposition of raw industrial features with ornate columns immediately adds visual interest to an interior space. The column's shaft might be fluted, carved with deep, even grooves along its length or left entirely plain. The capital is either intricately decorated with vine leaves in the classic Corinthian style or carved in the scroll-like form of the Ionic order.

8. Situated in a landmark building, this apartment in NoHo, New York, was previously converted by a rock musician. Now, as the home of a hedge fund manager and his gallery director girlfriend, it is a backdrop for their extensive art collection. Existing cast-iron columns painted white have a modern look.

9. This 186m^2 (2,000ft^2), open-plan loft in a former garment factory on New York's Lower East Side features original cast-iron columns and raw brickwork.

10.

10. This 279m² (3,000ft²) Greene Street loft in New York was cleverly configured by Slade Architecture as a series of spaces defined by new, 2.4m-high (8ft) volumes. Set along the apartment's length, these clever interventions indicate various living functions. One, a large aluminium bookcase holding a set of antique Korean trunks, marks out the living area, the kitchen and a dining space.

11. Arranging the loft in this way enabled the architects to retain the soaring cast-iron columns, which form a long, impressive colonnade. A custom-made table crafted from a single piece of timber takes centre stage in the dining area. The old industrial floor was stained, as a counterpoint to new elements. A tin ceiling, long lost, was replicated, to honour the loft's heritage features.

'Built in 1883, the space had great proportions and original details like cast-iron columns and huge windows. The scheme was designed to celebrate these.'

JAMES SLADE,
SLADE ARCHITECTURE

1.

SOARING
COLUMNS

TEXTILE FACTORY

Kortrijk, Belgium

This unique family home is situated in a former factory, just outside the town of Kortrijk in the Belgian province of West Flanders. GRAUX & BAEYENS architecten were commissioned to transform a single, 150m² (1,614ft²) space within the factory into a comfortable home for a couple and their child. The interior was constrained by two existing tall steel columns, which effectively divided it into two halves. Taking these columns as the central focus for the new scheme, the architects conceived a series of undulating walls and rooms around the perimeter of the principal living area, the curved, curtain-like forms complementing the rounded shape of the old columns and creating pockets of interest, light and soft shadow. The new construction sits upon a steel framework, which has been clad in plasterboard. The surfaces were coated in a delicately pigmented lime plaster; the finish has a tactile quality. The muted colour scheme adopted through the entire space – white and putty tones – creates a serene environment, in keeping with the industrial character of the building, and maximizes the natural light. Painting the old steel columns and vaulted brick ceiling shades of white unifies these structures. The soaring ceiling height enabled the architect to create rooms over two storeys, which are offset from each other. The large glass panes inserted into several walls afford a number of views of the double-height principal living area, where the placement of the original columns has been used to define the adjacent open-plan kitchen, dining and other living spaces. *graux-baeyens.be*

3.

'The scheme is an exercise in working with light. The undulating surfaces, inspired by the ceiling and columns, capture light and let it shift into shadows.'

BASILE GRAUX, GRAUX & BAEYENS ARCHITECTEN

1. The factory was built in red brick. Its strong linear design is Art Deco-inflected and characterized by imposing windows. Light floods into the loft through a set of four windows running along one facade.

2. Other than the freestanding breakfast bar, all of the kitchen units and utilities are set into the newly constructed walls, so that their long, sinuous lines remain unbroken. White cabinetry successfully forms a subtle connection between the new additions, the columns and ceiling.

3. The loft's incredible height is enhanced by two enormous columns. It enabled the architects to add nearly 93m² (1,000ft²) to the previous floor plan, with bedrooms at second-floor level offering dramatic views over the rest of the industrial conversion.

4. The original vaulted brick ceiling, now painted in white, provides an interesting textural contrast with the smooth plaster walls. Its form complements the old steel columns and the softer curvatures of the dramatic new architectural interventions.

BEAMS

Exposed wooden beams are a much-loved characteristic of converted Victorian warehouses, where the structural timbers were originally used to support pulleys for the unloading of cargo. By the 1790s, however, cast-iron beams and columns were appearing in multi-storey mills and factories. Iron had a greater load-bearing capacity than wood, necessary for supporting enormous machinery; in addition to being cheaper, it was also fire resistant. Today, by exposing original wooden beams, architects successfully enhance the unique industrial quality of a conversion as well as honouring the building's heritage. The timbers might even bear marks and scratches, wear and tear incurred during a previous, industrial phase. Heavily-beamed ceilings have a strong historic look, but can make living spaces feel darker, especially where ceilings are lower. Many architects and homeowners embrace this effect, leaving wooden beams untreated. However, whitewashing timber or staining it black will achieve a modern rustic style. Single beams, also a common warehouse home feature, offer similar possibilities and can serve to effectively frame spaces and views.

◀ Reclaimed beams inspired the design of the industrial-style staircase rising through three floors of this Lower Manhattan penthouse by ODA New York. Wooden handrails echo the beams, while wrought iron banisters subtly reference the beams' supporting metal joists.

1.

1. The trapezoid shape of this 279m² (3,000ft²) New York loft creates an exaggerated perspective in the living area – an effect enhanced by the tight-set exposed timber beams. Salvaged wood counters and the warm strip-wood flooring complete the space.

2. Jane Kim Design commissioned a blackened-steel canopy, directly influenced by load-bearing I-beams, that overhangs the open-plan kitchen and creates a dramatic, staging effect.

EXPOSED

Juxtaposed with bare plaster, concrete or brick, and reinforced by cast-iron or timber columns, a stripped-back, beamed ceiling emphasizes the industrial heritage of an interior and the very fabric of an old building. It is a compelling feature that many architects and homeowners are rightly keen to preserve. Warehouse windows and bare brickwork will enhance the impact of the beams. Exposing any original wooden flooring and using reclaimed wood furniture and cabinetwork will also maximize the historic appeal of ceiling timbers.

3.

4.

3. A parade of warehouses built in around 1863 in Shoreditch, London, was originally used by Patey & Co. Perfumers for storage and distribution. In 2013, Studio Kyson completed the conversion of one terraced property into a four-storey family home. Craftsmanship and heritage are celebrated through the original timber beams, offset by a strictly minimalist aesthetic. In the kitchen, low-hanging lighting draws the eye from the black counters to the wooden beams above.

4. Commissioned to transform an apartment in New Concordia Wharf, London, the first decision made by Inside Out Architecture was to expose the timber joist structure. The ceilings now define the unique character of the home. Lights inserted into plasterboard bulkheads meant the original joists remained untouched. White walls direct attention to the textures of the timber and brickwork. In this compact bedroom, simple decor ensures the heritage features are the key focal points.

5.

'This loft might be small, but it boasts a big-impact view. Painting the interior walls dark blue while keeping the end wall and ceiling white frames the window and enhances the impact of the original beams leading up to it.'

SHEENA MURPHY,
SHEEP + STONE

5. A compact apartment in a DUMBO warehouse in New York exhibits two individual, thick-set wooden joists that run the length of the living area. The pair of timber beams leads the eye to an incredible view of the iconic Brooklyn Bridge. Interior designers Sheep + Stone selected the 'Newburg Green' paint by Benjamin Moore for two of the walls, inspired by the metalwork of the bridge and the flowing waters of the East River.

6. The owners of this warehouse home in Portland, Oregon, wanted a sophisticated entertaining space. To achieve visual interest, Jessica Helgerson Interior Design painted the exposed wooden beams deep grey.

7. All-white beams and walls contribute to the sense of space in this former textile workshop in Barcelona.

8. In the bedroom of a London warehouse conversion, a white-beamed ceiling creates a tranquil environment.

BLACK & WHITE

Exposed wooden beams can make a room feel cosier and more enclosed. A dark grey or black stain will enhance this effect and is particularly striking against neutral walls. By contrast, painting beams a brilliant white creates the illusion of height and a much larger space by maximizing natural light. In former factories and warehouse residences, this is a simple treatment that softens industrial features – it is ideal for homeowners who prefer a contemporary, minimalist look.

I-BEAMS

Heavy-duty I-beams can span large spaces and bear incredibly heavy loads, so they are a structural feature common in warehouses and other industrial conversions. In some contemporary developments, they might be painted white or even a vibrant colour, but a more authentic industrial look is achieved if the original blackened-steel finish is retained.

9. A run-down Victorian warehouse in London was converted by Chris Dyson Architects in 2014 into this striking loft. The 220m² (2,368ft²) ground-floor loft apartment wraps around a new courtyard with a verdant planted wall. From the open living room area, the view of both the courtyard and the open-plan kitchen is framed by an enormous I-beam. This beam complements original brickwork in the kitchen and a polished concrete floor.

9.

BISCUIT FACTORY

Florence, Italy

T his unusual loft apartment occupies the entire attic floor of a nineteenth-century former biscuit factory situated on the edge of the historic city centre of Florence, Italy. The local architecture studio Q-bic conceived an unusual scheme for the 309m² (1,937ft²) living space, based on using reclaimed wooden pallets, which earned it the affectionate moniker 'pallets loft'. The unique, multi-functional space is primarily used for guest accommodation by its owners, but it has also provided a special backdrop for private parties and events. Pallets used throughout the loft – forming the sofa bases, bathroom unit and even a kitchen island – not only define its character but also inspire clever storage solutions. And, because much of the modular pallet furniture is mobile, the apartment can be entirely reconfigured with ease. Partial partitions, each painted in a different light grey tone, visually differentiate areas of the loft for various possible functions, while retaining the open-plan arrangement. Meanwhile, the vaulted, beamed ceiling, combined with the unrestricted floor plan, lends the space an almost church-like quality. The two ends of the attic are usually determined as sleeping or 'night-time' environments and can be separated from the principal living area by means of bespoke metal sliding walls. The soft industrial aesthetic of the 'pallets loft' is offset by a light and minimalist decorative scheme. Carefully selected items of furniture include design classics by figures such as Charles and Ray Eames and Le Corbusier, lending a subtle modern twist to the authentic heritage features. *q-bic.it*

1. Bare plaster walls and wood beams, combined with a pale concrete floor, create a serene backdrop to which industrial pallet furniture is well suited.

2. A Louis Poulsen pendant light hangs above the marble-topped Eero Saarinen pedestal table, creating an intimate dining area within an alcove.

3. Two tall stacks of reclaimed wooden pallets form a base for side-by-side bathroom basins. The space between the pallet slats can be utilized for storage.

4. A clever kitchen island, also fashioned from side-by-side stacks of pallets, is mounted on castors so that it can easily be moved for adaptive living. The soaring beamed ceiling is reminiscent of old churches.

'Stripping back the attic space to its raw components, soft plaster walls and light wood beams and joists, revealed the true character of the former industrial building. New skylights and an open-plan scheme ensure the entire heritage loft feels light and airy.'

LUCA & MARCO BALDINI, Q-BIC

4.

5. A generous aisle-like opening, running the entire length of the attic apartment, leads to a variety of adaptable living areas hidden within the recessed alcoves. The minimalist scheme features only a limited number of very carefully selected items of wall art, which include a composite picture in shades of blue, as shown here, which draws the eye in a space otherwise decorated in neutral tones. Wood-block side tables and stacked shelving reflect humble industrial forms and construction.

TRUSSES

The term 'truss' originates from the Old French word *trousse*, meaning 'a collection of things bound together'. In architecture and engineering, the structure serves a practical purpose: beams, joists and girders of steel or wood interlock to create a framework that supports the floor or roof above. Trusses usually take a triangular form or comprise a number of triangles, as this maximizes rigidity and transfers the load above most evenly. As this kind of construction can span sizeable expanses, trusses are particularly common in industrial buildings, where flexibility and the ability to create uninterrupted floor space for machinery and storage are essential. The planar truss, formed in a single plane, is most often found in factories and warehouses, where it is replicated in parallel groupings to support a roof; its soaring old wooden structures and complicated steel lattices continue to perform not just an aesthetic, but a functional duty. Trusses are, however, among the most dramatic and distinctive original features of industrial residences, adding unique architectural character to these homes and enhancing an impression of height and spaciousness.

◄◄ Boerum Hill house is a distinctive building in the heart of Brooklyn. Originally built as a warehouse, it was later repurposed as a church before its conversion by Delson or Sherman Architects PC. Heavy timber trusses stabilize the old building and recall its industrial heritage.

1. The home of developer John Parker Willis in Hyde Garage, San Francisco, was conceived by architect Erica Severns.

2. & **3**. Enormous steel I-beams brace the former industrial building at dramatic angles, intersecting with the heavy-duty ceiling and set against raw concrete walls.

FLOOR-TO-CEILING

Depending on their previous usage, some industrial conversions might display trusses anchored to the floor and ceiling. Whether made out of steel or wood, the scale and placement of these braces can be a challenge for architects and homeowners, particularly if redevelopment involves sectioning a space into separate rooms: on occasion, substantial structural trusses divide windows and entire living areas. There is usually an inventive architectural solution, however, and these impressive features can be used to set the tone for striking contemporary lofts.

'Our client's brief was clear: to uncover and celebrate the history of the building, preserve the raw concrete walls and enormous steel trusses, and offset these authentic industrial features with refined contemporary details.'

ERICA SEVERNS, ARCHITECT

4. Willis was responsible for the conversion of Hyde Street Garage, San Francisco, dividing the old industrial property into seven residential units and retaining one loft for himself. He stipulated white oak flooring, Carrara marble and a light colour palette for his 257m² (2,770ft²) apartment. In the bedroom, the understated decor in soft pastel tones ensures the huge steel truss built at a dramatic angle across the room, and the original, large factory window it transects, remain the focus. Line details in the soft furnishings serve to subtly echo the white, beamed ceiling.

ROOF

A shed structure, simply comprising a series of parallel trusses, is often employed in very large single-storey industrial buildings, as it maximizes floor space and creates height for machinery. Residential conversions retaining this feature are impressive.

5. Steel trusses span this 511m² (5,500ft²) water-cleaning station in pretty Villefranche-sur-Mer on the French Riviera, dating from 1910.

6. Owner Philippe Tondeur, pilot for Albert II, Prince of Monaco, sought help from interior designer Bernadette Jacques. It took fifteen years to complete the conversion.

7. The entire top floor of an old warehouse in Shoreditch, London, was converted into this photographer's residence. An open-plan arrangement enhances the sense of space and the visual impact of the timber-clad roof and trusses.

8. A vaulted ceiling with steel trusses spans the living area in this remarkable, four-bedroom lateral penthouse, sited on top of the Talisman Building in London's Hammersmith. It was sensitively converted by Gumuchdjian Architects.

9. & **10**. This old warehouse home in historic Bermondsey, London, offers a vast, 50-foot reception. A new minimalist interior ensures that industrial structures remain the focus. The entire area below one of the white-painted roof trusses has been fitted with a bespoke light-blue kitchen and storage cupboards that run almost the full width of the spacious loft. The bedroom is located on the open mezzanine above, between two trusses, and set behind frosted panels that let in light but provide privacy.

11.

WOODEN

Wooden trusses are prevalent in smaller industrial units built prior to the twentieth century and the development of structural steel. The warm tones and textures of original timbers add distinctive character to these conversions, often finished with wooden floors.

11. A complex latticework of timbers in this French warehouse frames industrial doors leading to a large outdoor terrace.

12. This former warehouse in Brooklyn served as a church before conversion into a home. Delson or Sherman Architects PC rebuilt exterior masonry and installed stabilizing timbers, which also recall the building's previous functions. A 6m-long (20ft) table of fir planks takes centre stage.

12.

13.

SPACES IN-BETWEEN

Soaring ceiling heights, common in industrial conversions, can be deliberately exploited for exciting new contemporary interventions. Considered storage solutions, mezzanines, and even structures like pods in unusual materials, might be inserted into the areas underneath and around trusses. Modern additions such as these contrast with heritage structures to create unique interior designs.

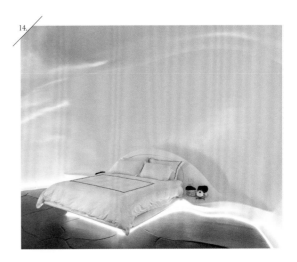

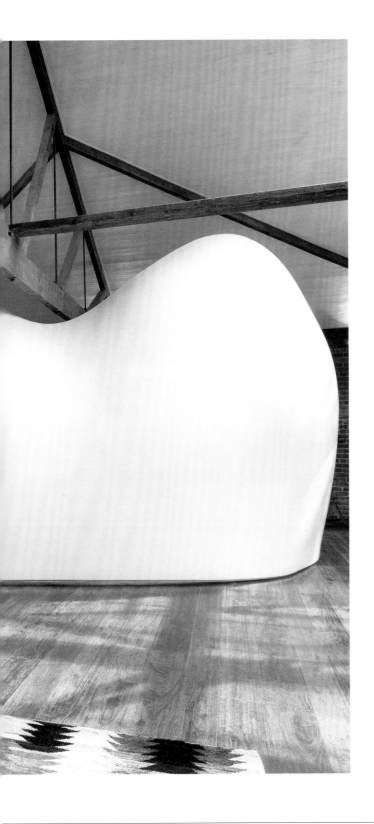

13. Architects Allen Jack+Cottier employed yachting technology to create this resin-coated pod at the heart of a former food factory in Sydney, dating from *c*. 1900.

14. & **15**. With all-white sculptural surfaces, the interior of the pod is almost other-worldly. A cocoon-inspired bedroom features soothing floor-level lighting. In the bright bathroom, a funnel form leads up to a skylight.

16.

'My wife and I built Paper Mill Studios together in order to realize our long-term dream of having our home, work and the people we love all together under one roof. This project has transformed all our passion and enthusiasm into the most incredible place to live and work.'

SAM ROBINSON, HOMEOWNER

17.

16. This loft studio is the realization of a long-held ambition for photographer Sam Robinson and his stylist wife Sarah. Working with Gresford Architects and Stack London Ltd, they injected new life into a former paper mill close to London's Old Street Roundabout. Original structural features frame thoughtfully conceived interiors, combining vintage and reclaimed elements.

17. A tranquil bedroom is secreted in the space between timber trusses, directly above the vintage-style kitchen. For Sam and Sarah, this is a live–work arrangement. The rest of the historic mill was transformed into photographic studios and creative co-working spaces. It's an intimate and inspirational setting that evokes the atmosphere of a stylish warehouse home throughout.

1.

2.

MODERN
MONOCHROME

WATER FACTORY

Melbourne, Australia

Situated in Fitzroy North, a suburb of Melbourne, this late nineteenth-century warehouse was refurbished and converted in 2014 by Andrew Simpson Architects. Over its long lifetime, the building has experienced many iterations: it has housed an aerated water factory, a jam factory, a modern engineering consultancy and an advertising agency. Today, it is home to a couple and their adult daughter. The Water Factory's footprint follows the boundaries of the site; as the building's heritage listing precluded any major interventions to the exterior, the residential conversion was primarily an interior project for the architects. The owners' brief required a highly creative response and focused on the provision of maximum flexibility, encompassing a wide range of evolving family living arrangements. Reflecting the many possibilities for adaptive reuse, the property's design was conceived as two side-by-side dwellings – one for the daughter and the other for the parents – both contained within the broader envelope of one building and connected internally via steel doors. The majority of the living spaces have been placed on the top floor, so that the ground floor can be utilized as required. While the architects' solution is contemporary and bright, with a strong monochromatic leaning, many original warehouse features, such as exposed brickwork and dark, stained wooden trusses, are celebrated throughout. It is that juxtaposition of traditional industrial and contemporary minimalist features that is absolutely central to the success of this distinctive, characterful family home. *asimpson.com.au*

1. The Water Factory's owner is an automotive enthusiast and he collects vintage Ford Mustang cars. This 1967 red convertible Mustang is the most cherished of his collection and takes pride of place within a six-car internal garage that is illuminated with salvaged 1970s pendant lamps.

2. The Victorian factory building's decorative brickwork is common to Fitzroy North. Two street-level entrances to the heritage-listed conversion – which provides dual accommodation in two adjacent homes – offer access for different family members and their visitors.

3. The bright entrance hall sets the scene for the heritage home's elegant monochromatic scheme. A limewash hardwood floor and white walls ensure the posts and beams of the interior remain the principal focal point. A new and beautifully crafted staircase sits in striking contrast with the original, black-stained beams and doors.

4.

'The ceiling geometry that varies and undulates along the cross section of the building conceals all of the electrical and mechanical services. It also provides an abstracted reference to the idea of houses contained within one single house.'

ANDREW SIMPSON, ARCHITECT

4. The first floor is dedicated to use by the parents. A minimalist kitchen is prominent, set against exposed brickwork, and appears to be a seamless continuation of the new, sectional ceiling design, where wave-like plywood panels intersect the original black timber trusses. The long, black hooded lamps echo the structural trusses. Beneath, the zinc-topped kitchen island completes the industrial tone and leads the eye to sliding glass doors and an outdoor deck.

5. A brutal 1980s first-floor extension, which had included an idle mechanical plant, was demolished in order to create space for a new outside area. A moveable kitchen island is ideal for summer entertaining and establishes a clever visual connection between interior and exterior spaces. The roof terrace has far-reaching views over the Fitzroy North suburb and Melbourne's skyline. It is bathed in light all year round.

5.

6.

'The sliding bedroom panels are a favourite feature. As well as serving a practical purpose, they add a sense of drama; pulling back the doors in the morning gives a lovely prospect of the rest of our warehouse home.'

HOMEOWNER

7.

6. To draw plenty of light and ventilation into an expansive space, operable skylights were introduced on both the north- and south-facing roof pitches. The strategic positioning of the staircase void ensures the enclosed ground floor benefits from natural light. Extending the concept of houses within a house, the architects conceived a neat design solution for the bathroom. A playful form, it resembles a typical house, with a pitched roof and 'front door'.

7. One half of the bathroom's pitched roof is glazed, filling the crisp white interior space with light while maintaining a visual connection with the rest of the loft and its old trusses.

8. The bedrooms, bathroom and laundry areas are divided by a series of white industrial-inspired sliding panels set on castors, providing flexibility. The main bedroom opens out to become a viewing balcony over the rest of the warehouse.

1.

◇ MODERN RUSTIC ◇

SILKWORM FACTORY

Spello, Italy

In the rural province of Umbria, 145km (90mi) north of Rome, stands a remarkable modern–rustic abode. This former silkworm factory turned tobacco-drying plant is more than two hundred years old. Abandoned for fifty years and severely damaged in the 1997 earthquake, it was still standing in 2008 but in dire need of renovation when it was discovered by hotelier Andrea Falkner and her publisher husband Feliciano Campi. The Campi family has published the famous Barbanera almanac for over a century; and for a publication devoted to country living, this factory's setting was ideal. The Campis converted two floors into offices and had a clear vision for the upper storey: an airy loft, offering open-plan living, with a separate kitchen and a bedroom.

Falkner had the right design experience, having decorated many other farmhouse and rental properties, but, at 492m^2 (5,300ft^2) and with a 9m-high (30ft) vaulted ceiling too, this industrial shell required professional input. Architect Paola Navone worked very closely with the Campis to preserve the factory's unique historic character while creating an inviting, practical home. A steel collar around the exterior walls was repurposed to hold up a gallery encircling the residence. A new partial wall separates the living spaces and bedroom. Fifty-two windows fill every corner with light, and the use of white against dark floors enhances the sense of space. The decor combines Navone's designs with vintage pieces sourced by the owners, chosen to complement the textures, scale, and authentic heritage of the property. *paolanavone.it*

1. A pair of leather armchairs on the mezzanine are a comfortable place to read and relax. The suspended fireplace mimics the industrial interior and creates cosiness in the cavernous space.

2. The sizeable white linen sofa taking centre stage in the living area was designed by Paola Navone for the Dutch brand LINTELOO. Industrial trollies on wheels serve as coffee tables.

3. The impressive 9m-long (39ft) dining table, which is central to the open-plan living area, was constructed from Kauri wood thought to be thousands of years old. Monochrome hexagonal tiles set into the wooden floor match those in the kitchen and cleverly define the dining area. A run of lantern-style lights hanging above the table create a dramatic scene.

3.

'The first consideration was the heritage of the place and how to fulfil the functions of living. Then careful attention was paid to natural light and selecting materials and decor to create a homely atmosphere.'

PAOLA NAVONE, ARCHITECT

4. The kitchen is the only part of the home that is enclosed. Metal-framed interior windows prevent cooking smells escaping into the living area, while still honouring the home's open-plan scheme.

5. Elegant floor-length white linen drapes softly screen a walkway that encircles the ground floor. The route is paved with geometric monochrome tiles, created by Navone for the manufacturer Carocim.

6.

'Paola Navone doesn't tend to work on private homes. But thankfully, once I had persuaded her to visit our former factory, she didn't hesitate to become involved. And she has realized our vision entirely.'

ANDREA FALKNER, HOMEOWNER

6. Woven Indian cotton drapes wrap around the iron-framed bed, creating drama as well as privacy. Clothing is stored behind curtains in double-height cabinets in order not to affect the minimalist look.

7. Reclaimed timber planks form a support for the bathroom basin. Exposed bulbs exert an industrial influence over Moroccan tiling.

8. A deep Bateau bath by Water Monopoly adds a vintage element to the bathroom, which looks over the pretty Umbrian countryside.

BRICKWORK

Red and brown brick characterizes many warehouse and factory homes, revealing the buildings' heritage and establishing a distinctly industrial background to the interior decor. An exposed brick wall, showcasing the very fabric of a property's construction, is a dramatic feature. From iconic London red brick to New York's distinctive brownstone versions, the ubiquitous building blocks lend colour as well as character. In fact, exposed brickwork is now so popular as an urban aesthetic that many modern homeowners are recreating the effect using realistic fake-brick panels and wallpapers. The visual repetitions of brickwork, and its tactile quality, can be complemented by a variety of contrasting materials. Raw brick, sealed but left exposed, can take a decorative scheme defined by bold colours and will contrast strikingly with concrete, wood and metal. For a rustic effect, brickwork can be whitewashed; alternatively, painting brick brilliant white will give a conversion a modern update, maximizing natural light and the sense of space while retaining the textural and visual interest of bricks and the pleasing effect created by their uniform shape.

◄◄ One of Düsseldorf's last surviving pre-war industrial buildings was redesigned to create a modern home by the architect Bruno Erpicum. Expansive glass walls and a minimalist scheme contrast with the original red brickwork, every detail of which is picked out by the natural light.

2.

RAW

Exposed brickwork can present many challenges: it might have to be professionally pressure-washed in order to strip back any paintwork and reveal the original brick underneath. It will then need to be sealed to prevent crumbling. But there is no question that, handled correctly, raw brick walls can be a triumphant feature in a residential interior, enhancing the sense of a building's former life. The tactile quality of aged bricks makes them a striking background for vintage furniture and accessories as well as modern fixtures and light fittings.

1. Art photographer Arne Svenson and his interior designer partner Charles Burkhalter reside in a converted caviar factory in New York's TriBeCa. The raw brick walls in their loft are offset by an eclectic yet carefully curated collection of vintage accessories, quirky creations and various taxidermied creatures.

2. Exposed brickwork in Tumblr founder David Karp's loft in Brooklyn, New York, provides the backdrop for a contemporary Niels Bendtsen for Bensen sofa and two Poul Kjaerholm leather chairs. The living area is situated on a raised platform crafted in reclaimed oak. The Jason Miller for Roll & Hill ceiling light is the ideal finishing touch in this sophisticated industrial space.

3. This former factory in the centre of Düsseldorf miraculously survived the numerous bombings of World War II and is now a contemporary residence. Architect Bruno Erpicum devised a minimalist treatment to maximize the drama provided by the brickwork. The kitchen is arranged in the exterior deambulatory, its glossed cabinets reflecting light and contrasting with the brick.

4. The family home of Marius Haverkamp, head of design firm Flow Works, is located in a former warehouse in the renowned Jordaan district of Amsterdam. The original, exposed brick wall provides a striking backdrop along the full length of the kitchen. Reclaimed timber cabinets, concrete work surfaces and a pair of black extractor hoods enhance the property's industrial aesthetic.

5.

BRICKS WITH PLASTER

Plaster of various ages, painted and raw, might be entirely removed to reveal the original brick beneath, but sections of it can also be retained. The lightly coloured stucco breaks up much larger expanses of red or brown brick and the contrast between the two textures and tones can add distinctive visual interest to a space.

5. & 6. A former cabinet shop and warehouse in downtown Auburn, Alabama, was converted by architect David Hill into a family home. The red-brick building, dating from 1920, was sensitively renovated while being transformed and adapted for the needs of his growing household. The original plaster retains the patina of different paint layers and has touches of glitter from the building's time as King's Kongo Klub. The cafe sign on the kitchen wall was salvaged locally.

6.

8.

BRICKS WITH TILES

More practical than brick, tiles are easy to clean and do not create as much dust. They are a particularly good solution for preserving walls that are chipped, crumbling or deteriorating. Tiled, at least in part, an old wall can be rescued in such a way as to retain its character without being plastered over. Subway tiles mimic brickwork in their shape and their smooth, high-gloss surfaces offer a strong visual and textural contrast with rough dark forms.

7. In the Stockholm loft of illustrator Sara Bergman, white subway tiles soften the effect of the brown brick walls and vaulted ceiling.

8. The tiled lower walls add a domestic feel to the former mechanical workshop and are a smart juxtaposition to monochromatic art.

9.

9. The defining features of the studio's open-plan live–work area are the crumbling, barrel-vaulted brick ceiling and walls, offset by white tiles, galvanized piping and a raw concrete floor. Mullioned windows and warehouse doors flood the space with natural light, while bulbs illuminate the studio in the evening. Work desks with trestle-style supports match the refined industrial aesthetic, and Bergman's flea market bargains add additional vintage charm.

10.

WHITE

Painting brickwork is often recommended as an easy DIY solution for either restoring or transforming interior brick walls, without the need for plastering, but bricks are hard-wearing and red or brown in colour, so this immediately dictates the paints that can be used, and paint is not always advised for brickwork that is crumbling or deteriorating. Where a suitable interior brick wall is painted, however, the effect can be striking. Shades of white, the most common choice, maximize natural light and enhance the sense of spaciousness while creating a clean, contemporary effect.

10. & **11**. In this 279m² (3,000ft²) loft in the former American Express warehouse building in TriBeCa, New York, SchappacherWhite Architecture D.P.C. used large panels of chemically treated steel to offset white brick walls and complement industrial columns. The materials' contrasting textures create drama in the residence, juxtaposing light with dark surfaces.

12.

'Painted raw brickwork brings out the character of the small ground-floor bedroom. Translucent glass panels, installed into the street frontage, protect privacy while drawing light into an otherwise narrow and awkward interior.'

GIDEON PURSER,
CHRIS DYSON ARCHITECTS

12. In this warehouse conversion in Shoreditch, London, painting the original brick walls of a long, narrow bedroom maximizes the natural light streaming through the feature window and creates the illusion of a larger space. The treatment ensures the industrial character of the room is retained. The chic bed by Timothy Oulton was inspired by F14 Grumman fighter jets. Aluminium plates and an aerodynamic design suit both the raw industrial heritage of the home and the bedroom's scale.

1.

CHARACTER
BRICK

CLOG FACTORY

London, UK

This Victorian clog-making factory in London had been used as a workshop and showroom by a fashion designer before its current owner, a filmmaker, commissioned Dow Jones Architects to alter the two top floors. The architects devised a solution that would preserve the heritage features of the old factory while, at the same time, transforming the existing rectilinear floor plans and generating new layers within the living space. The pitched roof was removed and replaced with twin oak boxes that span the original bare brick walls. Externally, this addition is clad with copper, in keeping with the industrial character of the building. Skylights set into the structure draw light into the building, heightening the interior spaces. Over the floors below, timber has been inserted to create a visual link to the rooftop intervention and serve as a textural counterpoint to the brick walls, which have been exposed with an almost archaeological precision. Concrete shuttered with oak tongue-and-groove boarding serves to add another warm tone and a texture to the understated interior scheme and further emphasizes the raw aesthetic of the old brickwork. On the second floor, home to the open kitchen and living room, original floorboards further add to the character, while the bathroom and bedroom on the first floor display the original, aged ceiling timbers. The simple interplay of just three materials – brick, timber and concrete – means that the building tells an authentic story of both its past life and its new incarnation as a place for reflection in the heart of a bustling metropolis. *dowjonesarchitects.com*

2.

3.

1. The former clog factory is set close to historic London Bridge and the capital's famed Borough Market, in an area that has seen significant recent gentrification.

2. Near the stairs leading up to the attic stands a mahogany and red leather chair from *c*. 1830–40. Old brickwork offsets an original work by the artist Mick Rooney.

3. The solid-oak dining table was sourced from Wales and crafted from a tree that had fallen in a storm. The three large, vintage factory lights in dark racing green were supplied from Trainspotters.

4. The concrete-framed kitchen cabinets were designed by Dow Jones Architects. Suspended down from the beams over the central kitchen island is a galvanized rail from which to hang saucepans.

5. The walls of the new addition are clad with beautifully finished oak, working in perfect harmony with the factory's rough old bricks. Exposed metal conduits on the walls add to the industrial look, which is enhanced by bare-bulb pendant lighting.

6. The architects designed layers within the residence, as a means of extending the rectilinear floor plans. Inserting the skylights added further height. Oversized sofas by George Smith, positioned under one such ceiling void, have a classic look.

'We took our clients to the Sir John Soane's Museum, the home and office of the eighteenth-century architect and collector. It is one of our favourite buildings in London – full of natural light, interest and intensity.'

ALUN JONES, DOW JONES ARCHITECTS

'It was important to us that any additions made to the building as part of the renovation were sensitive to the existing heritage features and the soul of the property.'

HOMEOWNER

7. The open-plan bathroom occupies the space beneath an original staircase and features a concrete floor and partial wall covering, framed by original brickwork and beams. Old train luggage racks form characterful, wall-mounted towel holders.

8. In the bedroom, wooden shutters and polished cast-iron radiators, sourced from salvage company LASSCO, complement exposed brickwork and replica windows. A charming antique wooden travel chest takes pride of place at the foot of the bed.

1.

MACHINE AGE

SHIP'S CHANDLER

New York, USA

When Rebecca Robertson and Marco Pasanella relocated to Manhattan's Southport, they were looking for a lifestyle change. Robertson had worked as an editor at *Martha Stewart Living* for over a decade. Her husband had enjoyed a successful career as an architect, author and designer, with work displayed in the White House and the Cooper Hewitt, Smithsonian Design Museum. They started their new lives with the purchase of a five-storey dockside warehouse. The building had been constructed in 1839 and originally housed a ship's chandler, a company making sails and maritime equipment. Later, it was used by a fish-trading company. The building, until recently, fronted the famous Fulton Fish Market, the bustle lending a unique ambience

to the situation. The surrounding neighbourhood is steeped in history; this was the first street on Manhattan to receive mains electricity. Today, at street level, visitors find Marco's fine wines store Pasanella & Son. The couple transformed the top floor of the building into their own home, where they reside with their son Luca, a pair of lovebirds and the family cat. For Robertson and Pasanella, it was most important to preserve the original floors, the exposed beams and timber columns; they valued the textures of the historic building and recycled as many of the original materials as possible. Painting the wooden floor in light marine paint, and the brick walls white, they gave the former warehouse a strikingly contemporary treatment, while also retaining the original language of the existing structure. *pasanellaandson.com*

1. The tiled chimney breast here is a subtle contrast to the white brickwork. The vintage tiles are Dutch, a thoughtful reference to New York's long immigrant history. Pasanella designed the central table.

2. Pasanella's book *Living In Style Without Losing Your Mind* suggests that real style is being true to yourself, not chasing trends. The couple's various pre-loved pieces add extra personality into the home.

3. The solid-wood kitchen island echoes the tone of the exposed roof timbers, while fitted open shelves, from floor to ceiling, are white and blend seamlessly into the exposed, white-painted brick walls.

4. The apartment features the original winch, once used to haul ships' equipment into and out of the building. Now it acts to define the play area within the context of the loft's wider, open-plan living space.

4.

'The area had been forgotten. It was 100 metres from Brooklyn Bridge, behind Wall Street and City Hall, by the water, somehow lost in time. We decided to make a life here.'

MARCO PASANELLA, HOMEOWNER

5. Fitted bookshelves enhance the sense of height in the apartment; a vintage library ladder on castors provides access to the high shelving. The white brick alcove beside the front door is the ideal place to hang both of Pasanella's vintage bicycles.

6. A new dividing wall separates the home into two distinct parts; an open-plan living area, with a family bathroom and separate bedrooms behind. White-painted brick walls and floorboards increase the sense of cohesiveness in the living space.

1.

LIVE
WORK

RAZOR FACTORY

Geneva, USA

Design duo Amy and Brandon Phillips live and work in this 6,039m² (65,000ft²), nineteenth-century factory. Having purchased the entire building in 2007 for just $137,500, over the years they have painstakingly restored this abandoned three-storey relic, with only a small budget but boundless creativity. Previously a straight razor factory, the building was humorously renamed 'The Cracker Factory' by the couple, who have a shared love of *The Simpsons*. A 61m-high (200ft) smokestack, which stands at one end of the building, is a valued feature of the local landscape. The Phillips' furniture company, Miles & May, now occupies the entire ground floor of the complex, with a workshop and showroom. The second floor comprises a 557m² (6,000ft²)

event space, several artists' studios and a 372m² (4,000ft²) letter-press workshop, which hosts regular classes. It also contains Amy and Brandon's two-bedroom apartment. The use of reclaimed and sustainably sourced woods is central to the ethos at Miles & May, for the creation of furniture Amy and Brandon describe as being both 'purposeful and prized'. In their loft, exposed brickwork sets the tone for a scheme defined by the extensive use of found objects and reclaimed materials. The continuous pitched ceiling, running the length of the space, was fashioned from maple flooring recovered from a factory in Michigan; it is clad in corrugated metal at one end, to define the bedroom area. It is the juxtaposition of raw brickwork and reclaimed wood with new, polished elements that is so successful here. *milesandmay.com*

1. The second floor of this red-brick former factory now houses artists' studios and a gallery space that can be hired out for private parties and wedding receptions. It is also a venue for 3stories, a non-profit hosting cultural events.

2. The 3m-high (9ft) heavy-duty doors, painted red on the outside, create a dramatic opening into the loft. The apartment is entered through the open kitchen, where marbled floor tiles contrast with partially whitewashed brickwork.

3. An open-plan arrangement ensures the factory's proportions and character can be enjoyed. In the living area, panels suspended from a truss beneath the 6m-high (19ft) ceiling act as room dividers and the backdrop for a selection of artworks. Two bedroom areas are situated just behind, while an enormous, vintage map has pride of place, forming the focal point for a custom-built shelving unit.

4.

4. The custom-made kitchen cabinets are cased in Carrara marble and the fronts finished in white automobile paint. They contrast strikingly with exposed brickwork and original windows. Painting sections of the raw brick walls white while leaving the other red brickwork untouched adds textural interest to the industrial space.

5. The Phillips often use their own home as a live space in which to test and modify their furniture designs. The May Rocker, handcrafted from walnut with a grid-like woven black leather seat and backrest, echoes the distinctive metal framework of 'The Cracker Factory's' large windows, to which coloured panes add a fun twist.

5.

6.

'We believe honest design, articulated through unique materials and impeccable craftsmanship, will stand the test of time. Our home, directly above the factory, is the ideal place to trial and finesse every new item.'

AMY & BRANDON PHILLIPS, HOMEOWNERS

6. Old, exposed brickwork defines the bathroom. The shower wall is finished in salvaged white marble offcuts. Reclaimed metal railway luggage racks hold folded towels.

7. Salvaged leaded windows and aged timber from the Coney Island boardwalk form the dividing wall and sliding door into the bathroom.

8. A bank of munitions cabinets sourced from a nearby army depot serves as a dividing wall between two bedrooms and offers plenty of storage. The space above the unit is open, retaining a sense of cohesion with the rest of the open-plan loft.

CONCRETE

Exposed concrete ceilings, walls and floors form amazing backdrops and emphasize the industrial character of a conversion, particularly when they are evident on a larger scale. The need to preserve original surfaces can influence the style and positioning of smaller details such as lighting, as well as larger architectural interventions, including staircases. But modern concrete surfaces can be introduced too. Exposed concrete will make a space look and feel colder, but this natural effect is actually beneficial in urban environments or hotter climates. Some homeowners embrace the raw aesthetic by contrasting rough and crumbling original cement with new, polished concrete details. Others find that adding a wide variety of textures – velvet and linen, natural timber and polished metals – to living spaces with concrete elements adds warmth and visual interest. Meanwhile grey concrete immediately lends itself to a minimalist and monochromatic interiors scheme, its softer tone is equally effective when juxtaposed with vibrant furnishings or pastel shades. Running throughout a residence, concrete expanses create a cohesive industrial style across all spaces.

◀◀ A pared-back colour scheme dominated by soft grey linens – with only a single splash of colour: a large green rug against the reclaimed oak floor – ensures that the raw-concrete ceiling is the defining feature of the bedroom in Tumblr founder David Karp's New York loft.

1. Exposed structural concrete defines this industrial conversion in Hong Kong by Mass Operations. Enormous windows afford stunning views across the megalopolis, while concrete interiors reflect the urban setting and achieve a raw, contemporary look.

2. The loft's owner is an art collector. The partial concrete wall divides the living area from the bedroom and acts as a canvas on which to display artworks and books. It also improves ventilation and light levels, with an unbroken view of the concrete ceiling.

FLOOR-TO-CEILING

The soft colour and tactile nature of concrete make it an interesting choice for extensive use throughout a residence; combining various finishes will enhance the visual effect. Stripping a conversion back to its basic construction materials will imbue it with a contemporary quality; such a treatment is ideal for those intent on a raw industrial or a minimalist scheme. In practical terms, large concrete surfaces create a naturally cool environment, ideal in urban and warm settings.

CEILINGS

In the decoration of homes, particularly modern residences, ceilings are often given little thought, but in many industrial conversions, the large-scale concrete ceilings are a dramatic feature that can radically influence lighting and decorative choices. Coffered concrete ceilings, comprising a series of sunken panels in square or geometric shapes, set a linear plan for the spaces below. Barrel-vaulted ceilings, common in continental Europe, conceal structural beams beneath an undulating decorative design. Every example creates a reason to look up.

3. Commissioned to redesign this loft in Clerkenwell, London, Inside Out Architecture stripped it back to its basic structure, revealing geometric ceiling beams. A modern lighting track complements the angular forms.

4. The barrel-vaulted concrete ceiling in this former printing house in Barcelona creates visual interest and enhances the sense of spaciousness. Sandblasted brick walls and towering columns contrast with the concrete.

3.

4.

5. & **6**. This apartment is one of three converted by William Tozer Associates in a former industrial building in London. The original, concrete ceiling structures extend throughout, unifying the spaces. Conceived as a series of highly rectilinear planes, this open-plan loft features new, dark timber columns and sliding panels to divide spaces, creating privacy for areas like the bedroom and concealing more functional spaces, such as the home office.

7. The pleasing contrast between warm timbers and cool concrete surfaces was fully exploited in this London warehouse conversion by Inside Out Architecture with the insertion of a floor-to-ceiling cabinet, which contains a work station.

8.

WALLS

Depending on the age of an industrial building, its original walls will likely be concrete. Leaving these exposed will immediately create a raw and contemporary backdrop against which modern monochromatic schemes, vibrant colours and traditional decor can all prove successful. This 'factory' look can also be created; for the most authentic result, walls can be re-clad utilizing pre-fabricated concrete panels which are bolted onto the existing structure. At the easiest, most cost-effective end of the scale, and a practical solution for any modern home, there are even realistic, digitally-printed 'concrete' wallpapers.

8. This loft in the Oriental Warehouse in San Francisco features double-height, site-cast concrete wall cladding. The grey is an ideal backdrop for the owner's collection of contemporary art and amazing lighting.

9. Concrete walls set a distinct tone in this striking industrial conversion by Michael Haverland. Walnut window trims reflect the dining table and flooring, and inject warmth, while framing New York's skyline.

10.

10. An old industrial building in the Barcelona neighbourhood of Gràcia has been converted into six separate residences. Their sizeable windows, bringing plenty of light into the living spaces, have enabled the bold and extensive usage of concrete panels.

11. Interior designer Katty Schiebeck used moody colours for these dwellings, heightening the dramatic effect of the broad concrete wall panels and flooring. In the bathroom, a large mirror over the vanity unit stops this from feeling oppressive.

12. Stained wood cabinets in the kitchen are a striking counterpoint to the lighter grey concrete flooring and walls. A wooden dining table and chairs add warmth, texture and curved forms to the more austere planes.

'We have always wished for a giant, hall-size studio: an empty space where we can lay hundreds of books on the floor. This abandoned factory offered that — as well as truly unique industrial aesthetics.'

ATTILA F. KOVÁCS, HOMEOWNER & DESIGNER

FLOORS

Whether a pre-existing feature or a recently installed covering, a concrete floor offers a full range of benefits. These floors are easily cleaned. They are naturally cool under foot in warmer climates or they can be heated from beneath. Polishing a concrete floor to a high shine is an industrial luxe treatment and also reflects the maximum amount of natural light, whether a conversion has expansive factory windows or includes darker interior spaces.

13. Originally built as a weapons plant in *c.* 1913, this complex later found a more benign purpose, as a knitting factory. For architect Attila F. Kovács and his wife, the art director and stylist Zsuzsa Megyesi, of A+Z design studio, a four-storey building within the neglected site was a chance to create a dream home. Polished concrete flooring in the dining room enhances the film-set-style industrial environments and reflects the light from restored windows.

14.

15.

14. The loft of Solenne de la Fouchardière is part of a former garment factory in London. Solenne is a partner in the furniture company Ochre, and her apartment combines vintage pieces with the company's designs. Concrete floors establish the loft's industrial aesthetic.

15. A subdued decorative palette was chosen by Technē interior designers to complement the industrial features gracing this warehouse home in Melbourne, Australia. Black steel details match the original windows, while concrete floors enhance the spacious feel.

16. This loft, set in the Wrigley building in Toronto, Canada, was completed by interior design practice Cecconi Simone. A polished concrete floor runs throughout and original warehouse windows remain. The interior is minimalist and calico curtains act as dividers.

16.

1.

CONCRETE
BRUTALISM

CEMENT FACTORY

Sant Just Desvern, Spain

Since founding his own practice in 1965, Spanish architect Ricardo Bofill has gained international recognition for projects built around the world. He designed his first residential project, a house in Ibiza, at the age of just seventeen. But it is a converted industrial complex situated on the outskirts of Barcelona, the architect's home for very many years, that is widely considered one of his crowning achievements. When Bofill discovered a disused cement factory in 1973, he saw a future for the partially ruined monolith that few others could even have imagined. The turn-of-the-century factory consisted of over thirty silos, echoing subterranean vaults and huge machine rooms. The remodelling work lasted two years; parts of the original structure were demolished to reveal sculptural concrete forms beneath and Bofill was keen to celebrate the very fabric and construction of the building. Once those structures had been defined, they were cleaned of decades of compacted cement and the interiors were entirely reimagined. Today, the former cement factory contains architectural offices, archives, a studio and exhibition space, as well as Bofill's personal residence and guest bedrooms. It is like no other residential conversion or office and serves as a true testament to the potential of former industrial buildings of all sizes. The complex extends over 3,000m^2 (32,292ft^2), of which 500m^2 (5,382ft^2) comprise the architect's home. Visitors, reportedly, often lose one another, but, then, what an astonishing and inspiring place in which to find oneself temporarily lost. *ricardobofill.com*

3.

1. The oldest cement factory in Spain, the now-retired grand, 100m-high (328ft) smokestack of La Fábrica is still visible from across the city of Barcelona. In addition, eight of the factory's thirty original silos remain after Bofill's extensive restoration, and together they give the property its distinctive, fortress-like character.

2. One of the world's foremost postmodern architects, Bofill has sensitively restored the brutalist Spanish cement factory, carefully preserving its soaring expanses and surreal concrete structures. Understated modern furnishings and decor, with select design classics, are all that is required in such a remarkable interior space.

3. La Fábrica's vast interiors, such as this – 'The Cathedral' – have a magical quality. This huge space, 11m (36ft) in height, is the factory's largest and serves as a magnificent venue for exhibitions, lectures and concerts. It is also an ideal gallery in which to showcase the architect's various detailed project models and drawings.

4. The huge double-height 'Sala Cubica' is a vast, cuboidal living space and the heart of the Bofill family home. The raw, exposed concrete walls give it an industrial quality, but the effect is softened by long, billowing drapes and the natural sunlight that is admitted through them all the year round.

5. The offices of Bofill's practice, Taller de Arquitectura, which employs a team numbering forty professionals, are accommodated in one of the restored, 15m-tall (49ft) silos. Once used to store cement, the space is now a hive of cutting-edge creative activity.

6. In this tranquil bedroom, a minimalist treatment that is characterized by white furniture and sheets ensures that the decor does not detract from the full drama of the rougher walls and ceiling. The unfinished concrete contrasts with the polished floor.

'To be an architect means to comprehend space. Here, spaces have been organized in accordance with mental activity rather than by the functions of more typical households.'

RICARDO BOFILL, ARCHITECT

7. Once surrounded by derelict yards, thick with old cement, today the former factory stands in the midst of abundant gardens, planted with tall swaying palms, eucalyptus, fragrant cypress and olive trees. Signalling the full transformation of the site, its towering exterior walls are now covered with established ivy and the industrial complex resembles a modern-day Babylon, both palatial and peaceful.

8. Bofill has masterminded many famous cultural centres in sites around the world, including the Arsenal Music Centre in Metz, France, and the Centro Cultural Miguel Delibes in Valladolid, Spain. But La Fábrica forms a dramatic backdrop for his own musical functions. The scale and the acoustics of 'The Cathedral' are ideal for the architect's private concerts and intimate soirées with clients or family.

DOORS

Industrial doors, often found in former warehouses and factories, combine practicality and authenticity. Originally constructed to withstand the heavy uses and abuses of industrial environments, the doors were more usually formed from metal and required little maintenance or replacement. Sliding doors on castors and swing doors on sturdy hinges provided easy entry and egress for the transit of goods and huge machinery being relocated. They were also often customized to fit very large or awkward openings and fitted with oversized bolts for security. Durable and reliable, even in abandoned and derelict buildings many industrial doors still survive. In a modern-day conversion, an original door will act as a distinctive feature and is likely to inform the decorative directions taken by interior designers and architects for the rest of the residence. Where old industrial doors are impractical or lacking, modern versions, particularly space-saving sliding designs, can be specially commissioned. Vintage or contemporary, a dramatic doorway is a striking solution for an entrance or room division that honours the building's heritage and enhances an industrial aesthetic.

◀◀ In a former shoe factory in London, a pair of metal fire doors dating from 1938 have been preserved and restored. The patination of the old metal and the detailing of the original mechanisms render this a captivating feature which inspired much of the conversion's decor.

1. A salvaged metal door in this Toronto loft slides open to reveal the bedroom behind. It also serves as a backdrop for select artworks.

2. The patinated metal door, comprising of riveted aluminium sheets and original fittings, is offset by large-scale, exposed metal ducting.

3. Many decorative details were inherited by the loft's owner. The Victor Vasarely prints in the bedroom are from her childhood home.

SLIDING

Evidence of sliding door tracks has been found in the ruins of Pompeii; this entryway construction has been a consistent feature of industrial architecture throughout history. The simple mechanism on running castors is easier to operate than a hinged door and enables the passage of goods and machinery. These doors also act as a safety mechanism, offering quick closure in the event of a fire. Today, even where an original model might not exist, sliding doors are popular in that they are space-efficient and have an authentic appearance, which instantly enhances any scheme's industrial aesthetic while remaining true to its origins. New doors can be crafted from scratch or, alternatively, constructed using reclaimed metal with patinated surfaces and bearing signs of wear and tear from previous usage, for a distressed look that is more in-keeping.

4.

4. This sophisticated loft in Chelsea, New York, conceived by BK Interior Design, combines the tone and refinement of a gentleman's club with both newly fabricated as well as original industrial elements.

5. A clever, space-saving solution, a sliding zinc door creates privacy for the calming master bedroom leading off the principal living area. The aged metal of the door is a visual link to vintage cast-iron radiators.

6. On the opposite side of the living area, another sliding door reveals an office-cum-guest bedroom. Tartan furnishings and a vintage trunk contrast with the dark-stained window frames and white-painted bricks.

'The large custom-designed zinc doors on runners are a nod to the building's original features, which include exposed brickwork and piping. They open up the space and bring extra scale and grandeur.'

BRAD KREFMAN,
INTERIOR DESIGNER

8.

7. A sizeable set of brushed zinc panels in the home of Solenne de la Fouchardière divides the principal living area from the bedroom but gives the option of creating a larger and more open space. The riveted sheets of metal have an almost stitched appearance – fitting for an old garment factory. This modern industrial addition to the loft apartment creates an impressive visual link with the building's authentic characteristics: large windows and concrete beams.

8. In this TriBeCa loft located in a caviar warehouse, Andrew Franz Architect created a dramatic dialogue between the building's original features and modern additions. Framing the entranceway, an industrial sliding door stands imposingly against the exposed brickwork and alongside a contemporary front door. The patination of the metal is dramatically offset by a new, red hallway closet. Timber from the old roof joists was repurposed as treads for the bespoke stairs.

'We paid close attention to the loft's surviving features and used the language of steel frames, concrete and brick to inform new architectural interventions, like this large sliding door, which blends seamlessly with the concrete-panel-clad wall as a striking industrial backdrop in the open-plan dining and entertaining expanse.'

ALBERT MO, ARCHITECTS EAT

9. Melbourne-based Architects EAT converted what was formerly a chocolate factory in the old industrial area of Fitzroy, Melbourne, into this striking family home. The 250m² (2,691ft²) residence was organized into a series of intimate spaces, with folding and sliding doors offering the potential to establish larger, open-plan volumes. High-ceilinged atriums and voids enhance the feeling of space and provide views of the sky. The building's existing industrial aesthetic has been complemented by sensitively selected new materials and interventions. In the dining room, a specially commissioned sliding concrete-panel door sits alongside brick walls and timber columns.

11.

12.

'We wanted to celebrate the original features of the former gas factory. Renovating the building for residential use, we decided to differentiate contemporary interventions. Bespoke glass sliding doors are modern in style yet reference industrial designs with telephone glass sucker handles.'

ZSUZSA MEGYESI, HOMEOWNER & DESIGNER

GLASS

Whether they feature clear panes or an opaque treatment, glass doors are an effective means of retaining a sense of spaciousness, allowing for plenty of light and establishing a visual link between different rooms and areas even when the doors are closed. In converted industrial buildings, glass doors create a design dialogue with original windows, and smooth planes of glass contrast strikingly with textured brickwork and concrete.

10. An attractive sliding door of frosted glass in a Budapest loft is a space-saving solution and enhances the flow of light. The new addition complements the reclaimed windows used for the internal mezzanine.

11. & **12**. In this former factory in Milan, a pair of practical, glass-paned doors preserve the connection between the kitchen and adjacent dining area, while providing the option of dividing them when cooking.

1.

THEATRICAL
SETTING

SHOE FACTORY

London, UK

A compact yet immaculately conceived apartment in a 1930s shoe factory in London's Clerkenwell is the residence of Dalia Ibelhauptaite, a director of opera and theatre, and Dexter Fletcher, who is a director of film and theatre. For this creative couple, architecture is akin to scriptwriting, so their brief to Angus Pond Architects was to transform the warehouse flat while preserving its authenticity and distinctive details, and to devise a home that was deeply personal. The couple's professions, extensive travel and family history all play out in this unique former factory home. It was the metal-framed warehouse windows that first attracted the couple to the property. Strangely, these had been largely obscured by a poor layout; the architects envisioned a new, open floor plan to ensure the windows could be fully appreciated on both sides of the building. Most of them feature the original metal rods and levers, which function together in unison – it is a beautiful and complex mechanical system that enhances the London property's industrial character and retains a sense of dynamic movement even when static. It was that possibility of constant change and motion that inspired a dramatic black 'magic' cube in the centre of the apartment, which serves as a personal archive and 'treasure chest', cleverly concealing the more functional spaces within. An original, heavy-duty fire door in the kitchen, complete with its old and highly articulated operating mechanisms, was the key inspiration for the use of raw-steel elements and a grey palette throughout the home. *apalondon.com*

2.

 'Dalia's grandfather ran a wood factory in a small Lithuanian town. During the full renovation, we found a tiny workshop in Lithuania and sourced two tonnes of oak for our walk-in wardrobe, desk and bathroom. It was a means of honouring our family.'

DEXTER FLETCHER, HOMEOWNER

1. There is a choreographed quality to this residence. At its centre, a black cube defines the three surrounding areas for sleeping, dining and relaxing.

2. Fletcher's great passion for architecture, which is regularly apparent in his film work, and Ibelhauptaite's set-design skills influenced the design scheme.

3. & **5**. Moveable black ash shoji screens evoke the couple's trips to Japan and complement the warehouse windows. They also bring a sense of theatre.

4. The sleek steel cube houses the bathroom. Its sliding raw-steel screens on the exterior walls conceal laundry facilities and a film and book archive.

6.

'Inspired by both clients' love of theatre and artistic clarity, the monochromatic palette was highlighted by the subtle introduction of light tones, industrial steel blues, rich dark olive green and unexpected textures.'

ANGUS POND, ARCHITECT

6. The only details remaining from the factory's past were its windows and a set of metal fire doors dating from 1938. The sturdy industrial features informed materials and colours used throughout the residence. A Poliform kitchen with dark-grey granite surfaces was specially commissioned to suit this industrial look.

7. The perfectly formed open kitchen is an elegant stage for entertaining. A trio of hand-blown glass globes provide direct light for the dining table and create a theatrical atmosphere. The preserved fire doors were repurposed to conceal a new, ingenious cupboard, with shelving that houses the couple's glassware collection.

EXTERIOR WINDOWS

One of the most attractive features of factory and warehouse conversions is usually considered to be the windows. Often very large, they flood the interior spaces with natural light. It was for this reason that the loft-living movement of the 1990s was driven by artists and the creative community. Architects and homeowners embarking on the conversion of old industrial buildings will often need to replace the existing windows, either because they are broken or only single-glazed. If the property is protected by a heritage listing, its authentic character must be recognized through the installation of modern replicas. Steel-framed windows in particular have experienced a surge in popularity in recent years due to the influence of stylish warehouse conversions. They were first used in the mid-eighteenth century, when the Industrial Revolution made steel more widely available, but significant improvements in manufacturing practices have now made factory-style windows a practical choice too. There is no doubt that such windows, whether they are original or contemporary additions, can serve as dramatic and aesthetically pleasing architectural features in a property.

◀◀ In the Paris loft of Daniel Rozensztroch, artistic director of lifestyle brand MERCI, the tall factory windows flood the kitchen with sunlight. The steel finish is complemented by a classic Tolix table and Mathieu Matégot perforated-metal shelves, enhancing the industrial aesthetic.

1.

'It was the expansive Crittall windows that set this apartment, in a former east London factory, apart. We added simple white blinds to offer privacy when needed while ensuring the original windows could be enjoyed in full.'

NIA MORRIS, INTERIOR DESIGNER

1. Interior designer Nia Morris entirely reconfigured this loft apartment in London to create two bedrooms and an open-plan living space. Original factory windows run down two full sides of the large kitchen–living area, bathing the entire residence in natural light. The steel window casements establish the tone for a clean, almost monochrome scheme, which, in combination with white-painted walls and concrete ceilings, emphasizes the sense of airiness. The Douglas-fir, wide-planked flooring is a practical yet smart update for this modern industrial conversion.

METAL

Steel window fenestration is high performance and low maintenance; the framework is durable and capable of holding very large panes of glass. Because the metal frames are extra slim, typical factory-style windows also maximize natural light. Steel is weather resistant and can be left raw or powder-coated in various colours (although black is the traditional choice). With the rise in industrial renovations, these windows are also enjoying a renaissance in architecture more widely, giving commercial and residential projects alike a distinctive finish.

2.

2. Built in 1926 for BFGoodrich tyre company, this San Francisco warehouse was redeveloped into lofts in 1996. The owners of this apartment had downsized from a more traditional home, and chose to commission a local architect, Cass Calder Smith, and interior designer Vaughan Woodson, for the industrial loft's remodelling. Their joint solution enclosed two bedrooms and master bathroom within the core of the apartment, while the open-plan showpiece living area is defined by original features, including the huge old warehouse windows. A neutral, timeless scheme contrasts with the industrial frames and rough, exposed concrete walls and pillars.

3.

4.

WHITE-FRAMED

Whereas black window frames add a certain dramatic flair to a residence, white windows, by contrast, seem to create a more seamless connection with the exterior and with views. White-framed windows are also particularly powerful when combined with brickwork or concrete that has been painted a brilliant white, for a contemporary, gallery-like living space.

3. The windows on three sides of this Art Deco industrial building offer unobstructed views of Manhattan. SheltonMindel designed a run of cabinets underneath for storage and art displays.

4. This old aeronautical factory in London was reworked by Trunk Creative. In the open, social kitchen, glass-brick windows were preserved and throw sunlight across the industrial space within.

5.

IN THE ROOF

Original and newly added skylights in the pitched roofs of older industrial buildings flood the ample and double-height spaces with sunlight, while emphasizing the spectacle of sloping roofs and architecturally interesting or enormous interior volumes. The feature can be particularly impressive in properties with galleries or mezzanines, which offer the opportunity to create raised living areas, full of light and providing a space for retreat.

5. In the Shoreditch home of Solenne de la Fouchardière, sloping windows draw light into an intimate living room. A heavily worn concrete truss reminds guests of the building's industrial past and adds further visual interest to this quiet corner of the apartment.

6. Designers Isabelle Puech and Benoit Jamin converted a French carousel workshop into a 350m² (3,767ft²) live–work space. Vintage furniture and flea market finds offset industrial features. Very large skylights in the roof create a serene mezzanine for rest and reading.

7.

8.

'It was our responsibility to dance around the old existing structure and to celebrate the inherent beauty of its heritage features. It was clear to all involved that this would still be a laundry at the end of the day. We were preserving the building's story and simply writing a new chapter.'

CHRIS HAWLEY, ARCHITECT

PIVOTING

Factory and warehouse windows are often characterized by functional mechanisms. Heavy-duty windows which either pivot open in their entirety or feature a tilting panel are simple to operate. They offer an effective means of adjusting the levels of ventilation in a space and have the added benefit of being very easy to clean from the inside.

7. A tilting hangar door is the only original window in the Fargo Laundry by Chris Hawley Architects. It was repurposed for a porch and modified with a motor and track. All of the other windows in the conversion are new, high-performance, triple-glazed windows copied exactly from the old frame pattern and operation from 1915.

8. The porch is adjacent to a bar with a hanging beam sculpture, used for gatherings throughout the year. Existing concrete floors were polished but still show oil spots from heavy-duty machinery.

WOODEN

Timber window frames will add to a warehouse conversion's authentic historical character. They are more traditional in appearance than steel frames. Whether original, or modern replacements that are modelled on old fenestration, wood that is left unpainted is ideally suited to former industrial buildings featuring brick and timber ceiling beams or floors.

9. The sizeable open-plan living area of this penthouse apartment in a New York warehouse was formerly used as an artist's studio. Timber-framed windows on the western and southern exposures fill the space with natural light. The effect is further enhanced by 5m-high (17ft) ceilings and white-painted brickwork and beams. A steel-and-glass wall was conceived by The Turett Collaborative to partition off the master bedroom without compromising the light.

1.

WOW-FACTOR
WINDOWS

FLOUR MILL

Denver, USA

The Longmont Farmers Mill was built in 1920 and played a central role in Denver's old flour milling industry for four decades, but the consolidation of the industry forced the closure of the mill and by 1975, only the shell of the building survived, quickly falling victim to vandalism. Of the original sprawling complex, only the mill building and three storage bins now remain. The conversion of the historic structures into lofts was completed in 2000 and brought new life to the flour mill once respectfully dubbed the Pride Of The Rockies, as well as prompting a proliferation in industrial conversions across downtown Denver. This sizeable apartment was remodelled by local architecture firm Robb Studio, working together with Chicago-based Studio Gild. Its owner had originally planned to reconfigure only the laundry room and the guest bathroom. But an initial search for new cabinet hardware quickly grew into a desire to transform the entire loft. The original industrial features, including galvanized piping and overhead ducting, exposed brickwork and concrete, are complemented by a sophisticated decorative scheme and understated palette. Interior designers Studio Gild focused on honest materials, combining custom millwork with mid-century and vintage finds. The original flooring was given a soft grey finish that connects with the concrete walls and achieves a modern look. An open-plan approach ensures that the impressive, 4m-high (14ft) ceilings and large factory windows with their 270-degree views remain the defining features of this airy and light-filled home. *studiogild.com*

1. The light-grey contemporary kitchen blends seamlessly into the raw concrete walls. Custom-built grey-stained cabinets are finished with counters in white macauba quartzite, while the wall-mounted units are clad in perforated metal.

2. The open-plan 279m² (3,000ft²) loft is ideal for entertaining, and the dining area, situated adjacent to the raised, stage-like kitchen, is marked out by a deep-teal rug and a dramatic, industrial-style chandelier in front of the window.

3. Architects Robb Studio utilized the mill's original chimney stack and conceived a modern fireplace in concrete and steel to sit within. The hearth seat was crafted from oak charred using the distinctive Japanese Shou Sugi Ban method.

 'Two considerations were the loft's incredible views of the Rocky Mountains and its remaining industrial features.'

JENNIE BISHOP, STUDIO GILD

4. The custom vanity unit in the bathroom is crafted from oak charred using the Shou Sugi Ban technique and topped with a 15cm (6in.) carved-marble slab-sink. The tube wall lighting, designed by Michael Anastassiades, completes the bold and masculine aesthetic.

5. A freestanding vintage clawfoot bath with modern faucet sits in front of an enormous black-framed window, with dramatic views of Denver and the Rockies. Photography by Alex Prager, part of the owner's modern art collection, offsets the raw industrial textures.

5.

1.

ARTIST'S
RETREAT

TEXTILE FACTORY

Como, Italy

Architect Marco Vido ran his eponymous practice for twenty-five years before making the decision to take a new creative direction and pursue his passion for painting. Today, he paints almost full time, devoting one day per week to architectural work. His atmospheric live–work loft in an old textile factory on the outskirts of chic Milan is the perfect place in which to indulge this artistic passion. Vido has retained the industrial building's broad open spaces, which are ideal for the large canvases on which he paints and absorb the natural light streaming through the preserved factory windows. Working in graphite, oils, acrylic and bitumen, he mixes many of his pigments by hand. Splatters of these now combine with the traces of textile dyes still visible on the walls and, together,

they create a unique backdrop to an otherwise sparsely decorated space. The architect–artist was overjoyed when he came across the abandoned and empty 269m² (2,900ft²) factory, a rare find in Italy. Eager to preserve the original dimensions and character of the factory as far as possible, Vido made few structural alterations. Wooden flooring was laid throughout and half-height walls surround a bathroom, but the concrete ceiling beams and iron-framed casement windows are original, and the rough, unfinished walls have been left untouched. In this way, Vido has drawn directly on Soviet constructivism and the functional style of Rationalism, both of which are evident in Como's architecture, and has preserved the factory's distinctive, raw industrial appeal in creating this remarkable live–work space. *marcovido.com*

3.

1. The 1920s textile factory is set near an abandoned railway in Como and every window offers a distinctive vista of an imposing industrial landscape and forms.

2. A minimalist platform bed and two side tables, all designed by Patricia Urquiola, are set in front of an abstract artwork on a sizeable canvas painted by Vido himself.

3. & **4**. Plasterboard panels painted grey and black divide the principal living area from the bedroom and bathroom. This common construction material honours the industrial features and allowed the architect to avoid making any significant physical alterations to the factory shell. Half-height walls ensure the bathroom enjoys light from the expansive windows.

'Architecture is a beautiful thing, but it is always for a client. With painting, the client is me. This unique building has enabled me to indulge both my passions.'

MARCO VIDO, ARCHITECT

5.

6.

5. This stainless-steel kitchen island is ideally suited to the building's industrial aesthetic and its polished surfaces reflect the light streaming through iron-framed factory windows. The long kitchen table was handcrafted from fine chestnut wood based on a design by Vido himself, and is surrounded by black-lacquered Hans Wegner curved-frame Wishbone chairs.

6. The long desk was custom-made from marine-grade plywood and is utilized by Vido and his two sons. The unit is the perfect height for desk-based work and it benefits from plenty of natural light, set comfortably beneath large windows. The folded-plywood Benjamin stools, a classic IKEA design, slot neatly under the desk and suit the factory's functional look.

7. A sandstone platform is used as a studio space by Vido. The exposed concrete walls behind, still splattered with textile dyes from the factory's former life, now create an unusual backdrop to the artist's oversized canvases. They establish a colourful connection between past and present.

8. The floor space in front of a huge factory window serves as an informal library, while the sill is used to display favourite collected items. Sunlight streams in through these enormous windows all year round, though the architect acknowledges that they can also sometimes let in the winter wind.

INTERIOR WINDOWS

The huge open spaces offered by former factories and warehouses are appealing, but partitions are usually needed to establish functional living areas. Newly created interior spaces carved out from larger volumes often lack windows in their exterior walls and require an alternative solution in order to benefit from natural light and air. Glazed internal windows are an ideal solution, drawing plenty of light into these enclosed areas while, at the same time, enhancing the sense of open-plan living so prized in large-scale industrial buildings and literally framing existing heritage elements. Rather than creating isolated zones, interior windows increase the sense of cohesiveness and visual connection between different areas of a home. Whether a single-glazed door or an expansive, wall-to-wall feature, these interior windows can be impressive in their own right. Metal casements are an effective means of referencing original factory windows, while wooden frames will create a more traditional look and ensure any new addition is still in keeping with a building's existing elements. Glass that is frosted or opaque creates seclusion, its matt finish contrasting with a darker frame.

◄◄ In this London loft by Mark Lewis Interior Design, a newly created interior wall features glass panels and a paned door. These internal windows, while isolating the master bedroom, preserve the sense of open-plan living and ensure the concrete ceiling remains entirely visible.

1.

1. This nineteenth-century gas factory, located in Budapest, was converted from an abandoned shell into a home by A+Z Design Studio. It overlooks the Danube River on one side and industrial buildings on the other. Crittall-style windows, found on site, run the full length of the interior.

2. Enormous factory windows and high ceilings fill the conversion with natural light. Flowing white drapes draw the eye towards the view and create a theatrical backdrop for an eclectic mix of vintage and contemporary furniture designs and a dramatic centrepiece red pendant light.

FLOOR-TO-CEILING

The full drama of double-height urban lofts can be significantly increased with the insertion of full-height interior windows. The feature is a clever way of creating new interior spaces on two storeys within the existing volume while retaining a sense of openness in the rest of the residence. At floor level, a continuous run of windows might incorporate a glazed hinged or sliding door, providing a convenient entryway and a seamless finish. Meanwhile, a floor-to-ceiling treatment also cleverly conceals the insertion of a second floor or mezzanine. These newly created rooms situated on upper levels offer a bird's-eye view of the apartment below.

3. A trio of glossy black Notte pendant lamps by Prandina hang over the Gray dining table by Gervasoni, drawing the eye to the former factory's double-height windows. The various mismatched chairs surrounding the dining table were each selected for their 'unique personality' and bring visual interest to the space, but the factory windows remain the focal point.

4. In the first-floor home office, the full window wall offers direct views over the bedroom below and the Danube River. The reclaimed windows connect heritage and modern. A simple desk with a trestle frame is a nod to the building's industrial past and is paired with a simple vintage school chair and Prouvé cabinet by Vitra. White surfaces further brighten the space.

5.

BLACK-FRAMED

Black steel-framed fenestration is an effective way to bring light into the deeper recesses of old industrial conversions while retaining the authentic character of the building. The steel frames can be very thin, supporting large glass panes and spanning large expanses. This ensures that the overall effect of the black frames is not oppressive. Painting any exposed brick white and adopting a monochromatic interior palette will further enhance the drama of interior windows.

5. Melbourne-based Architects EAT transformed the renowned MacRobertson chocolate factory in the city's Fitzroy suburb into a light-filled family home. A crucial amendment to the building's existing architecture was the addition of steel-framed interior windows. This new feature fills the entire building with sunlight.

6. Interior windows run full height and along the length of the main bathroom, ensuring a relatively narrow space feels bright and airy. The black frames enhance the industrial aesthetic in a space that otherwise featured only a small section of the original brickwork. They also emphasize the steep pitch of the glass roof.

7. This charming study is located in a former caviar warehouse built in the 1890s and converted in 2005.

8. Dash Marshall design studio recreated the office of the caviar company's boss in homage to the loft's past.

9. A panelled door and frosted windows offer privacy while providing a link to the rest of the New York loft.

WOOD-FRAMED

Wooden window casements, doors and joinery immediately imbue a space with a heritage look. Whether lightly oiled, painted or stained dark, the tactile nature of wood adds to the character of industrial conversions featuring exposed brickwork. Wooden window frames complement old timber beams, columns and flooring. The use of traditional fixtures, including brass, will ensure a sophisticated finishing touch.

1.

2.

BEAUTIFUL
BI-FOLDS

PRINTWORKS

London, UK

The Factory was one of the very first warehouse conversions in London and was named by the developers after Andy Warhol's infamous New York studio. The building was actually originally an Edwardian printworks, and was then used as a storage depot for The British Museum before finally being converted for residential use in 1999. Units were sold off as shells and are therefore unique internally, though the current owner of this loft had to see beyond a poor layout put in place by the previous resident. He was keen to create a flexible new living arrangement and re-establish the loft's dramatic proportions. He also had a strong desire to use reclaimed material throughout. Having previously purchased vintage industrial light switches from salvage expert Mark

Rochester, he knew that Mark could source unique original materials, and, over a number of months, the two worked together closely to source and select furniture and various accessories. A full set of folding, antique glazed panels, salvaged from a church, were a key factor in the complete reconfiguration of the loft space, creating the possibility of separate living areas yet allowing light to flow throughout. The wooden flooring in the bedroom and in the living room is original. Laminate wood in the rest of the apartment was ripped out and it took six months to source a suitable pine floor (from a former factory) with which to replace it. Due to the age of the building, metal conduits had to be run over the exposed brickwork; early twentieth-century bulkhead lights and switches complete the look. *rochesters.uk.com*

 'The use of Victorian glazed doors creates a range of dynamic possibilities, with the option to create different combinations between the areas, and the flexibility to open the space up. They also contribute vintage character.'

MARK ROCHESTER, INTERIOR DESIGNER

1. A long apartment with large windows at each end was modified, through the use of pitch-pine glazed doors from a Methodist chapel in Yorkshire, to create several interconnected living spaces. Stepped kitchen and bathroom platforms bring dynamism to the layout.

2. Glazed doors can be folded back to connect both the living area and bathroom. Films projected onto any of the white walls can then be enjoyed from the restored late-nineteenth-century French zinc bath. Alternatively, concealed blinds on the doors can be drawn for privacy.

3. The negative of the bathroom and the dressing area forms the kitchen recess. The long island is a vintage haberdashery counter; an old Glenister draughtsman's chair serves as the bar stool. The Victorian blackboard, sourced from a Lancashire school, is for shopping lists.

4. A bank of turn-of-the-century metal deed boxes still bears clients' names and is an unusual storage solution.

5. A salvaged glazed library bookcase with sliding doors and brass handles was reconfigured to fit the extractor.

6. The large steel cabinet in the bedroom is Strafor and originates from France. It would have been used as a shoe locker in a factory. Today, the metal unit acts as a low-level room divider as well as providing additional storage. It complements the metal window, which has a pivoting centre panel.

7. A vintage Singer machinist's stool stands in the dressing area, in front of a Victorian drapier's cabinet that contains clothes and shoes. A mahogany library ladder leads from the dressing area and bathroom to a partially concealed raised sleeping platform, which is accessible through a small portal.

'Almost everything that has been introduced is old. This gives the space a real sense of soul. The bi-fold doors create intimate spaces within the larger envelope of the loft.'

PAUL ALLTON, HOMEOWNER

1.

RAW
INDUSTRIAL

UPHOLSTERY FACTORY

London, UK

When interior designer Mark Lewis was invited to fully renovate an empty 186m² (2,000ft²) space in an old London upholstery factory, the brief was to create a luxury two-bedroom apartment that retained authentic industrial features. Timber flooring installed in the 1980s had been laid over bitumen. Stripping it all back revealed original Victorian floorboards, which were painstakingly salvaged and relaid on the surface. The concrete and steel-panelled ceiling adds a distinctly raw aesthetic overhead. These striking features, and the dramatic proportions of the old factory, can now be fully appreciated as a direct result of Lewis's open scheme; the designer avoided compartmentalizing the space. Where new, essential internal walls were inserted, interior windows at ceiling height draw in the light while offering a continuous view of the distinctive ceiling finish. A pared-back aesthetic and simple palette further ensure the original characteristics of the building are truly celebrated; the reclaimed roofboard, quarry tiles and galvanized conduits enhance the existing textures. There is a continuous sense of belonging and of the building's working history. In contrast with the industrial elements, honed marble, solid brass and bronze hardware contribute a refined feel, sitting against raw brickwork and concrete. Modern additions to the home include a perfectly conceived pantry with climate control, but the overriding impression is of a past life captured and vintage elegance achieved in the very heart of east London's fashionable and youth-oriented Hoxton scene. *marklewisinteriordesign.com*

1. In the open kitchen, signs of the original paint have been left on a brick wall, to create an authentic distressed appearance. Bespoke cabinetry was finished off with Carrara marble countertops. A vintage, wooden pot cupboard is an ideal base for the ceramic sink; an Aston Matthews solid brass tap is a chic finishing touch. The old loading bay doors were re-hinged and are now double-folding.

2. A traditional pantry means the kitchen is uncluttered. It is lined with white subway tiles and fitted with reclaimed timber shelving on cast bronze brackets to hold pots, pans and groceries. Climate controls are ideal for storing wine.

3. The factory's concrete ceiling was sandblasted to remove years of paint and reveal the steel joists. The imprint of timbers used in the construction of the ceiling adds to its textural quality. The open-plan layout and internal windows ensure this ceiling can be enjoyed throughout the home. The floating shelves were created from old joists found under the flooring, and zone the apartment without blocking the flow of light.

4.

'Our scheme exposes and celebrates the authentic textures and raw structures of the former factory. The simple, honest aesthetic celebrates its heritage as a working space.'

MARK LEWIS, INTERIOR DESIGNER

4. In contrast to the industrial living space, the bedrooms have a rich, sophisticated look with velvet curtains and sisal flooring. Old cast-iron radiators reflect the origins of the building and Dowsing & Reynolds wall lights cast light on smart tongue-and-groove wall panelling painted in an elegant Prague blue.

5. Robert Kime wallpaper with a traditional print adds warmth to the bedroom. An old service lift in the far wall was uncovered and cleverly repurposed as a walk-in wardrobe. The old doors were re-formatted to open out and oversized brass handles salvaged from a London pub add a masculine finishing touch.

6.

 'I wanted a home that was at once comfortable and inviting while retaining the essential characteristics of the building.'

HOMEOWNER

6. A Drummonds shower with oversized head and traditional taps adds character to the master bathroom. Reclaimed 23cm (9in.) Welsh quarry tiles, used only in the bathroom, create a visual character distinct from other spaces, while an integrated timber shower tray connects neatly to the other wooden flooring.

7. The hardwood throne toilet was designed specifically to fit in the space. It extends into a bench with concealed compartments for toilet paper and magazines. The new interior walls, created using brick slip, match the former factory's original brickwork.

8. An Aston Matthews bath takes pride of place in front of this window, which required only light restoration but was updated with new bronze hardware from Frank Allart. A simple white rollerblind is ideally suited to the unadorned aesthetic. A Fritz Fryer wall lamp had its shade removed for a more industrial feel.

STAIRS

One of the principal challenges in converting former industrial buildings is their increased floor to ceiling heights. Another can be the need to ensure some original surfaces, particularly those protected by a heritage listing, including concrete floors or exposed brickwork, remain unbroken. Such unconventional volumes and heritage features will often demand bespoke solutions in a residential conversion. Architects try to find opportunities to use contemporary interventions as a means for creative expression and as clever counterpoints to original features. A staircase, be it unadorned or highly stylized, becomes much more than a solution for ascending from one living area to another: from cantilevered to curved steps, with plain or patterned treads and balustrades, there are a number of important decisions to be made as regards scale, proportion and finish. Industrial materials and processes are an effective way to reference a building's past. In double- and even triple-height spaces, stairs become dramatic focal points, visually unifying different storeys. Even in compact areas, stairs can rise to the challenge, creating dialogue between old and new.

◄ A former munitions factory in Mulhouse, France, is the home of Anne Hubert, founder of online store La Cerise sur le gâteau. The steel staircase, designed by architect François Muracciole, emphasizes the loft's monumental proportions and original industrial aesthetics.

SPIRAL

A centuries-old architectural device, the spiral staircase is a space-saving solution. The construction can fit into compact areas or serve as a freestanding structure, always maximizing floorspace. The iconic corkscrew form, with wedge-shaped winders fixed to a vertical central support, can be crafted in a variety of materials.

1. This 1930s industrial building in the Mission district of San Francisco was originally a warehouse for Lucky Strike cigarettes, but later housed an auto-repair shop and a software company. Artist Clive McCarthy bought the 929m² (10,000ft²) warehouse in 2006 and commissioned Natoma Architects to transform it. Their soaring spiral staircase is easily the most dramatic feature, suspended from the roof and hovering above the concrete floor.

2. 1990s additions to the warehouse were stripped back to reveal its original features, and the clever juxtaposition of rough and smooth differentiates those old, raw elements from the building's interventions. A walkway with a perforated-steel balustrade runs around the two-storey volume's interior, linking workspaces with living accommodation, while a cavernous central void maintains the dramatic scale and proportions of the industrial building.

SCULPTURAL

The grand dimensions of an industrial conversion can be one of its most impressive characteristics. In such sizeable spaces, simple, sculptural forms can be especially dramatic. In stair design, a strong minimal line or sweeping, curved form can naturally enhance the impression of movement, transition and discovery when ascending through a building.

3. An old warehouse conversion in Sydney's sought-after Paddington suburb features this slick staircase solution. Baker Kavanagh Architects designed a black steel I-beam handrail to reflect other existing features.

4 & **5**. A loft in a former butter factory in Melbourne was given a futuristic remodelling by architect Adrian Amore, who conceived a sleek modern staircase that twists and turns upwards. It was tested and constructed on site from steel, then covered in plywood and plaster.

6.

U-SHAPED

U-shaped staircases comprise two parallel flights of stairs between successive floors, connected by an intermediary landing positioned perpendicular to both. They can be left- or right-sided and, over several storeys, two or more sets of these stairs might combine to form a single, imposing structure. As the upper floors of a building always remain concealed, U-shaped arrangements maintain the privacy of upstairs accommodation, separate from the lower floors.

6. This former brewery cooperage is believed to date from the 1900s. Chris Dyson Architects extended its basement laterally to create an open living space that opens into a triple-height atrium.

7. The very elongated flue of a floating fireplace and a spectacular blackened-steel staircase complement the exposed red-brick wall and emphasize the soaring height of this unique London conversion.

8.

9.

MINIMALIST

Sometimes simple really is best; a slimline staircase can be just as visually powerful as a more complex creation. Blackened steel is the ideal material for any space defined by exposed brick and concrete, offering a contemporary counterpoint to these heritage features and a dramatic silhouette. A lack of adornment belies the architectural challenges and design considerations behind a minimalist staircase feature, however. Steel is folded and welded to create light-seeming and delicate staircases, which still have innate structural strength.

8. Concrete, brick and steel combine to great effect in this home. Viewed from the side, a wafer-thin black steel staircase becomes a single plane. The solid side doubles as the balustrade, ensuring original brick is untouched.

9. In an overhauled gearwheel factory in Amsterdam, a razor-sharp steel staircase unfolds, origami-like, from the first floor to ground level. While the metal treads and risers make a material connection with the I-beams above, the staircase's light, linear design is also a striking counterpoint to those heavy-duty architectural features.

1.

FAMILY
FEATURES

INTER-WAR FACTORY

London, UK

This large, triplex family apartment is set in an inter-war Jackson & Joseph factory in the heart of London's East End. The building underwent conversion in the 1990s and was used for some time as a studio by the artist Tracey Emin before being purchased by the current owners. For the family of two adults and their four children, the key consideration was the creation of flexible and functional spaces with fun touches and plenty of integrated storage space, but preserving the gritty industrial features of the building was also considered essential. The ground-floor entrance is approached via a narrow courtyard and characterized by original steel-framed windows. The large basement kitchen was upgraded and minimally modified; it links to an inviting, open snug area.

Vitsœ shelving was fitted in the long first-floor corridor, in order that this otherwise underused space could double as the children's study. The bedroom overlooking the entrance yard was divided in two and ingeniously fitted with bespoke high-level children's beds with storage below. The master bedroom received new built-in wardrobes, and toilet and shower compartments. Two essential elements enhance the factory's industrial character: a resin-coated concrete floor unifies the spaces – heated from beneath, it is at once sleek and practical, yet not too cold. A new staircase, which links the three storeys, combines understated plywood cladding with an elegant, ribbon-like steel balustrade. Fans of the artist can look out for an original crayon graffiti by Emin on the same wall as this new staircase. *chrisdyson.co.uk*

2.

1. The steel-frame window and front door at the entrance to the home fill the spacious hall with light, an effect which is amplified by the polished concrete flooring.

2. The large basement kitchen was upgraded but only minimally altered. Pale wooden furniture was deliberately selected to offset the plywood-finished staircase.

3. Combining plywood treads and risers with thin steel banisters and handrail, the industrial-style staircase complements the riveted steel columns, which have been painted white for a more modern look. The stair materials contrast pleasingly with the concrete floor.

4. & 5. The ground floor received three joinery interventions, which included a cleverly conceived wall panel and concealed fold-down bed providing overnight space for occasional visitors. There is also a study on castors, which is easily relocated within the living space.

'With young children and regular guests, we needed a flexible, open-plan family home. White walls maximize the sense of space. Concrete floors enhance the building's distinctive industrial character.'

HOMEOWNER

SERVICE

MEZZANINES

Factories and warehouses are constructed at an entirely different scale to most public buildings, in order to accommodate large machines and offer plentiful storage, with expansive floor space and soaring ceilings. Converting these monolithic industrial constructions for residential use, architects have two options: to embrace the double-height expanses, or carve up those great volumes into smaller, more amenable living spaces. A mezzanine is, in some respects, an architectural compromise: a means of creating pockets or platforms for private and practical quarters while celebrating the cavernous proportions of old industrial properties and retaining the sense of open-plan living. Areas for sleeping, relaxing or working, sometimes even bathing, can be accessed via a showpiece staircase and might be partially enclosed with screens or windows, or simply encircled with a balustrade, to maintain the connection with the rest of the accommodation. Mezzanines benefit from a bird's-eye view over a home, yet are removed from the bustle of the main living areas. They are very often awe-inspiring architectural features in their own right.

◄◄ In the 9th arrondissement of Paris, a former industrial workshop once used for repairing carousel horses is now the distinctive home of two fashion designers. A mezzanine above the old office, now used as a kitchen, has been painted black to counterbalance the old brickwork.

2.

FREESTANDING

1. Firm adn architectures inserted two freestanding towers into this former shoe factory near Brussels, creating new interior spaces while still preserving the overall scale and rough concrete ceiling of the space.

2. A laundry room and bathroom on the ground floor both have doors. But the mezzanines atop the towers, reached by folded-steel staircases, feature perforated metal screens which let in daylight while maintaining privacy. Used for sleeping and working, the mezzanines are also open to the original ceiling.

In some spaces with characterful original features such as brickwork, concrete ceilings or wooden trusses, particularly those protected by a heritage listing, a self-sufficient new structural intervention is a clever solution. An open-topped tower ensures the full scale of larger, double-height spaces can still be appreciated, while creating smaller interior areas for living on the ground floor and a private mezzanine above, with 360-degree views covering the rest of a loft apartment.

MINIMALIST

A mezzanine with a minimalist design will add a contemporary edge to a former industrial building, heightening the sensation of light and space, while ensuring original features remain the focus and can be enjoyed from a lofty vantage point. Simple lines, including pared-back balustrades, and a limited palette of materials and textures, will ensure the mezzanine blends seamlessly into its surroundings.

3. Airhouse Design Office put a huge white box at the heart of this converted warehouse in Yoro, Japan. Inside, it contains a bathroom painted lime and the master bedroom in purple.

4. The mezzanine area, used as the children's room, is open to the high, vaulted ceiling and large family living area below, taking complete advantage of the building's old proportions.

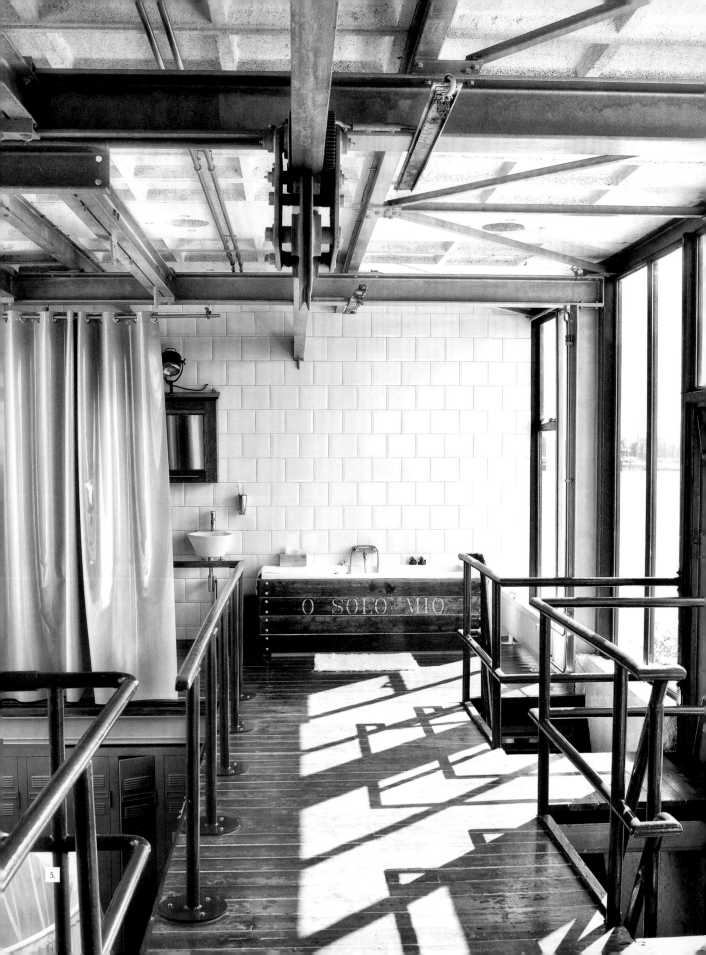

5. This harbour-side industrial conversion in Rotterdam has a raised metal gangway leading to an open mezzanine for the bathroom. White subway tiles and reclaimed wood offset the original pulleys and I-beams.

6. & **7**. The home of David Karp, the founder of Tumblr, is surprisingly low-tech. Set in an old warehouse conversion in Williamsburg, New York, it is a tranquil retreat for a tech entrepreneur. Original brick and concrete were the starting point for the full renovation by Gachot studio. Situated up on the mezzanine, the bedroom is only partially enclosed, while a freestanding bath offers views of the loft below. Steel railings reflect the building's industrial heritage and original features.

METAL

In former industrial buildings, blackened steel and cast iron emphasize the existing structural features. Metal railings and balustrades are the ideal pairing for galvanized conduits and piping, structural I-beams, columns and metal window casements. Mezzanine features that are finished with heavy-duty metal railings cleverly mimic the loading gangways that are common to factories.

2.

BRILLIANT
BROWNSTONE

LIQUOR WAREHOUSE

New York, USA

Remarkably, the current owner of this 1,301m² (14,000ft²) triplex purchased the entire building on eBay. After the unconventional acquisition, he commissioned leading firm ODA New York to redevelop the nineteenth-century warehouse into three unique apartments, a five-bedroom triplex and a street-level store. The five-storey warehouse is situated in what is now known as the TriBeCa North Historic District, occupying a long and narrow site that is just 7.6m (25ft) wide. Commissioned in 1892 by liquor merchant Joseph H. Beams, it was the first of several warehouses designed for Beams by architect Julius Kastner. The Romanesque Revival-style warehouse was subsequently secured by a pistachio baron and, later, an artist, but fell into disrepair.

Following decades of neglect, the beautiful terracotta-and-brownstone brick facade was painstakingly restored by ODA. Round-arched windows topped with terracotta mouldings, decorative cornices and capitals with foliate details were among the original features preserved. The old sidewalk vaulting was uncovered and the former cast-iron facade reinstated at street level. Metal fire shutters on one side of the building were reproduced for the other. The new rooftop penthouse was added, inspired by the elevator and stair bulkheads typical of historic New York warehouses and old industrial buildings. Clad with standing seam zinc, and with steel windows and railings, the modern addition is now the crowning glory of a historic TriBeCa building sensitively restored back to its former splendour. *oda-architecture.com*

1. In accordance with the rulings from the Landmark Preservation Commission, ODA New York extended the existing brick-built bulkhead to ensure that the new 93m² (1,000ft²) pavilion on the rooftop of 10 Hubert Street was concealed from street-level view.

2. New structural additions such as a striking steel and frosted-glass walkway reflect the building's historical context, most notably the area's distinctive, nineteenth-century cast-iron architecture that used to dominate TriBeCa.

3. The dramatic steel walkway rims the living area and serves as a library. The building's interior brickwork was largely intact and required only light patchwork. It is now best admired seated in the impressive double-height space.

3.

4.

'The penthouse has a masculine air, reflecting the building's industrial past. The use of steel, glass, wood, and a sparing use of colour mean authentic elements still do all the talking.'

ERAN CHEN, ODA NEW YORK

4. In clear contrast to the living area, the bedrooms are largely plastered and painted white. Brickwork adds visual interest, texture and colour and is also complemented by a window seat made of reclaimed timber.

5. The steel-framed shower enclosure is in eye-catching contrast to the elegant grey marble surround and mimics the industrial-looking windows introduced into the penthouse.

6. Built in 1892, the former liquor warehouse features heavy-beamed ceilings. New wall-to-wall windows in the traditional Crittall style and dark wood flooring perfectly complement heritage timbers.

7. Full-height, bi-fold doors with glass panes maximize the flow of natural light into the penthouse. They can be opened to create a seamless link between the interior and the expansive roof terrace. The far-reaching view from the patio incorporates contemporary high-rises and former industrial buildings sited nearby. This is a striking juxtaposition that echoes the successful integration of all the modern elements into this heritage warehouse conversion.

1.

MEZZANINE
DRAMA

TOY FACTORY

London, UK

Photographer Dean Rogers commissioned Sadie Snelson Architects firm to transform an existing warehouse conversion in Clapton, east London. Prior to the renovation, the property had been plagued by a number of issues: it had failed to function efficiently as a living space, having been clumsily subdivided into several disjointed rooms. Dark, dingy and airless, condensation collected inside the windows and the conversion also suffered from damp. The architects created a clean canvas from which to work by removing most of the dividing walls as well as parts of the floor. This immediately created a dramatic, double-height, open-plan living area, the scale of which once again paid homage to the building's industrial past. As Rogers often has to work from home, the flexible space now incorporates a series of smaller private rooms, including an office, which are set neatly along one side of the warehouse conversion. But the 'hero' feature of the scheme is the substantial new first-floor mezzanine. The contemporary open-plan kitchen with concrete island sits in the recess beneath. Above, clad in acid-washed metal, the imposing structure cantilevers out beyond the original steel columns supporting it and over the living–dining areas. To maintain a distinction between this mezzanine and the pre-existing columns that are adjacent to it, it is suspended by a rod from the ceiling rather than being locked in to the uprights. It has the effect of a royal box overlooking a stage and is itself the theatrical centrepiece of a light-filled live–work space, ideal for its creative owner. *ssarchitects.co.uk*

1. Sadie Snelson designed a new concrete island for the white-tiled kitchen, to complement the old industrial conversion. It was cast by the client, who also acted as the contractor on the renovation.

2. The materials and finishes that were used throughout the project were selected to reflect its past. Exposed plaster walls were left unpainted and the steel I-beams define the home's dimensions.

3. The new Crittall-style windows add further drama to the internal elevations and enhance the flow of natural light, while preserving privacy. A home office for the photographer owner is enclosed behind double-height windows on the ground floor, with crinkle glass utilized for the lower panes. The study door blends seamlessly with this full-height room divider.

4.

'We wanted the new structural elements to be as distinct as possible from the existing features, yet complementary to the industrial heritage of the building.'

SADIE SNELSON, ARCHITECT

4. Viewed from the side, the specially commissioned folded-steel staircase and balustrade take on the appearance of fine line drawings. The delicate look belies their sturdy construction.

5. The new interior fenestration mimics the original black steel warehouse windows and offers privacy as well as a view over the double-height living area.

6. In the bathroom, the double shower is finished in tadelakt, a waterproof Moroccan plaster traditionally used in hammams. The mottled grey tone contrasts effectively with the soft, salmon walls seen throughout the rest of this industrial conversion. Frosted-glass interior window panes screen off the bathroom while still admitting natural light from the open-plan home.

URBAN OASES

One of the greatest challenges of city living is finding any green space; it often feels as elusive as one vacant seat on public transport. But, just as unique and unusual residences have been created from clever industrial conversions of all kinds, so architects and homeowners are focusing their attention on crafting pockets of greenery and garden spaces of various sizes in the very heart of the city, from balconies for quiet contemplation to expansive terraces that make for breathtaking entertaining spaces. Look up from any New York street, and you might just spy the top of a tree or two, signalling secret rooftop gardens high among the city's iconic water towers. Some residential conversions have been reconfigured to enable the inclusion of secluded internal courtyards, carved out from the buildings' existing footprints. Colourful flower beds, verdant planted walls and paved patios contrast with urban surroundings. In other suburban settings, former loading bays and yards might afford even larger spaces for creative architects to conceive landscaped gardens, and buildings that once vibrated with noise and activity now invite rest and relaxation.

◄ The terraces of Rotterdam's iconic Jobsveem warehouse are among its most attractive features. Dramatic concrete overhangs offer shelter in inclement weather and shade from the sun's full glare, while the impressive industrial doors connect the interior and exterior spaces.

1.

INNER COURTYARD

Where a former industrial building fills an entire site, from boundary to boundary, architects face significant difficulty when trying to create new open-air spaces. One solution is to remove sections of original roofing to create an internal courtyard, concealed from street view and using at least one of the original perimeter walls as a decorative backdrop to planting. Trusses, the skeleton of the old building, can also be preserved.

2. Inside, the skylights and long bench seating form a visual continuation of the open-air terrace features, and create the sense of a seamless link between the indoor and outdoor areas. Exposed, soft red brick-work in a sunlight-filled corridor provides an ideal environment for artworks.

3. Daylight floods in from the internal courtyard and into the main living area. The decor is minimal and enhances the brightness and airiness, but wooden furniture, together with accent pieces in shades of green, make a decorative reference to the wooden trusses and pretty, planted courtyard space outside.

1. For bg architecture, the challenge of this warehouse conversion in Australia lay in maintaining the integrity and character of heritage features, such as trusses, while inserting a new north-facing courtyard.

4.

5.

4. & **5**. Corben Architects converted an empty warehouse in Sydney into this unique modern home for a couple and their three teenagers. The site presented several challenges, including a heritage listing requiring the retention of the roof trusses. The greatest issue, however, was that less than 15 per cent of the enclosing walls opened onto external spaces. A new indoor courtyard, emphasizing the truss form in its shape, brings sunlight and fresh air into the living areas and the bedrooms. Sizeable bi-fold doors mean that the entire space can be opened up. Remote-controlled awnings can also be retracted to increase the light levels in this atrium.

6. This warehouse conversion in the desirable Sydney suburb Surry Hills cleverly combines new interior and exterior architecture within the original perimeter walls to form a striking residence. Built in 1910, the red-brick warehouse later served as a transport hub, political club and nightclub. Outside, there are few clues to the transformation within, but stepping through an industrial front door, guests enter a series of angular spaces and find intimate corners, like this cosy reading nook.

7. The home of an art collector, a consideration for this project was the need to control light, airflow and climate, in order to preserve the owner's distinctive collection of furniture and art, as well as a need for calm. New, white-painted walls establish a gallery-like aesthetic. A tranquil inner courtyard, meanwhile, creates a soothing place in which to admire the juxtaposition of new and old.

GARDEN

Outdoor space comes at a premium in any urban environment, and former industrial property requires a visionary architect to create an inviting retreat. Careful attention to detail creates a meaningful connection between the heritage architecture, new interventions and the exterior landscape. But former loading bays and yards can then be transformed beyond recognition.

'Demolition was a consideration as the building was in poor condition. But our client was committed to preserving its industrial character.'

*JON CLEMENTS,
JACKSON CLEMENTS BURROWS ARCHITECTS*

8. The former Golden Crust Bakery in Melbourne, Australia, was fully refurbished in 2009 by Jackson Clements Burrows Architects. The family home now sits within an expansive garden and architectural landscaping complements a heritage building.

9. & **10**. A bridge was conceived as a way to connect two primary living spaces and to establish a social link between the teenagers' rooms in the outbuildings and the main residence. On sunny days, this sculptural walkway creates a shaded retreat within the garden.

11.

11. Built in 1897, The Spratt's Works in east London was once the world's largest dog food factory. One of London's first residential warehouse conversions, it was turned into 150 live–work units in 1985 and over the years residents have included the tapestry restorer to the Queen and the *Spitting Image* creator Roger Law. Today, the former factory is home to a thriving creative community. These pictures were taken by a resident, the photographer Debbie Bragg.

12. Outdoor spaces are particularly prized in London, even on the city's outskirts. The Spratt's Works offers private terraces, balconies and a large communal roof garden for residents, which is concealed from ground level. This delightful, walled English country garden is accessed via a garden gate beside Bragg's apartment. Complete with its potting shed, trees and rambling roses, it is an unexpected discovery on the factory's rooftop and an inviting retreat after a day in the city.

ROOFTOP

Factory and warehouse rooftops would rarely have been used, other than for building services such as water storage. Today, however, some of the most exciting industrial conversions provide communal gardens and private rooftop terraces for use by residents. While these high-up, open-air spaces can offer panoramic views of the city, and impressive backdrops for both quiet contemplation and entertaining, they are also often entirely concealed from street-level bustle. Naturally, these retreats are particularly desirable on warm summer days and clear nights.

13. New York's city skyline is dotted with rooftop water towers. Most buildings taller than six storeys will require a tank (usually wood) to provide adequate water pressure for tenants. Their forms are best admired from the roof.

14. Real estate developer Matthew Blesso worked with architects Andrea Steele and Joel Sanders to create a 204m^2 (2,200ft^2) eco-friendly garden above Blesso's 297m^2 (3,200ft^2) two-bedroom penthouse in Lower Manhattan. A walkway over the penthouse bulkhead, planted with herbs and wild flowers, leads to a 3m-high (10ft) meditation platform with a 360-degree outlook.

15. The rooftop is clad with hardy, Ipe wood decking and the silhouette of the open-air shower mimics other industrial elements. An inviting seating area beside a stainless-steel kitchen is ideal for summer entertaining. Swaying grasses and trees soften the exterior walls and create a green oasis in the heart of the city. A trumpet vine is a backdrop for a projector screen, if guests can tear their gaze away from the city and East River views.

15.

16.

17.

'Originally completed in 1913, the former warehouse Jobsveem is a national monument. When converting it for residential use, it was essential that we preserved interior and exterior features.'

ROBERT WINKEL, MEI ARCHITECTS AND PLANNERS

BALCONY

Outdoor space of any size is prized in urban environments and even a small balcony can transform an apartment. In former factories and warehouses, old loading bays might be transformed into sweeping terraces or balconies, with the important addition of new balustrades for safety. In other residential developments, windows can be added or expanded to accommodate new, steel-framed balconies that will complement the industrial building's existing features. Flowers and balcony furniture contrast with heavy-duty concrete, brick and steel.

16. Set on Lloyd Pier quay in Rotterdam, the Jobsveem warehouse demonstrates construction methods that were actually very advanced for their time, such as the stacked structure, with concrete galleries and loading bays. This design cleverly protected stored goods from the elements.

17. Jobsveem was converted by local firm Mei architects and planners in 2007. It now comprises a community of over 200 residents. Heavy loading doors still define the building's unique look and bring industrial character to spacious balconies at the front and rear of this building.

1.

HANGING
GARDEN

CAVIAR WAREHOUSE

New York, USA

The heritage of a former caviar warehouse in TriBeCa, New York, was an immediate source of inspiration for local firm Andrew Franz Architect. The 279m² (3,000ft²) loft on the top floor was fully reconceived as an expansive entertaining space, with its original features celebrated and a seamless connection with the outdoor environment created. The warehouse was built in 1884, and many of its structural characteristics – the arched windows, exposed brick walls and timber beams – were preserved. Vintage furnishings contrast with the industrial character of the space. New additions, including cabinets and metalwork, were custom made by local craftsmen. A specially commissioned steel staircase, featuring wooden treads fashioned from ceiling joists that were salvaged from the warehouse roof, leads to a mezzanine, which was relocated and glazed to create a dramatic, enclosed, sunken courtyard. The glass roof of this hanging garden is retractable and further steps ascend to a rooftop terrace above, filled with colourful native plants and with spectacular views of New York and the Hudson River. The suspended sanctuary is another architectural triumph, successfully integrating the outdoors into the main living space. The 14m² (150ft²) retractable skylight draws plenty of fresh air and natural light into what was previously a dark and poorly ventilated apartment and, in the evening, the softly lit hanging garden takes on the appearance of a large and very leafy lantern; this calming space serves then to gently illuminate the apartment below. *andrewfranz.com*

3.

1. The rooftop terrace is fully paved in re-purposed bluestone and features an abundance of colourful, low-maintenance plants, which act as a natural insulation. The views of New York are remarkable.

2. A retractable, flat glass roof over the suspended courtyard creates a seamless connection between the open-plan living space and the rooftop terrace above. It fills the home with light and the interior courtyard functions as a natural sun trap.

3. A large, teal-green sofa takes centre stage in the impressive double-height living area, continuing the theme of bringing the outdoors in. The striped floor rug mimics exposed beams above.

4. In the dining area, the bare brickwork serves as a striking backdrop to the simple lines of the mid-century modern furniture designs. The red brick complements the warm tones of the timber and offsets the crimson leather upholstery and green rug.

'Embracing the old building's industrial past, our scheme creates a visual discourse between new and old, devised through the juxtaposition of restored or reclaimed materials and contemporary additions.'

ANDREW FRANZ, ARCHITECT

5. An expansive new interior glass wall maintains the airy and open-plan expression of the loft. Heavy-set timber frames create a theatrical perspective on dramatic double-height bedrooms, set back to back, and offer a direct view of their original, raw brickwork and windows. These are features that can also be appreciated from the custom-made upholstered bench seats. A warm colour scheme and sophisticated decor complement the tones of the exposed brick, while dramatic lighting draws the eye to the timber-beamed ceilings.

1.

SECRET
GARDEN

CANDY WAREHOUSE

Sydney, Australia

This twentieth-century industrial building had, over the years, been used as a warehouse by Oh Boy Candy Company, before becoming a cane and rattan factory and, later, housing a furniture manufacturer; it had no external land originally. In 2013, Virginia Kerridge architecture firm were commissioned to transform the abandoned building into a family home. The exterior of the warehouse was stripped back and its more recent blue-painted rendering removed to reveal the brickwork beneath. Throughout the extensive renovation, as many materials as possible were retained and recycled: timber and bricks were saved and cleaned to be re-used. But arguably the greatest transformation came with the architects' intelligent solution for retaining the impressive

scale of the old industrial site while also creating a unique suburban oasis. To facilitate the insertion of a north-facing, private courtyard garden into the building's existing footprint, part of the warehouse roof was deconstructed. The garden's proportions are based on the golden mean, and it is framed by original structural features. This new addition informed the rest of the conversion and is the anchoring feature for the entire home. The lush, green space is visible from most areas of the residence and gives a sense of cohesion, filling the property with fresh air and natural light. The ground floor contains the children's bedrooms, which have direct access to the garden, while the master bedroom, family rooms and kitchen are situated above, with views onto the peaceful courtyard and a long, wooden deck with pool. *vk.com.au*

Dundrum Library

Items that you have checked out

Title Warehouse home : industrial inspiration
for twenty first century living
ID DLR27000045734
Due: 06/02/2023

Total items 1
Account balance 0.00 EUR
16/01/2023
Checked out 1
Overdue 0
Hold requests 0
Ready for collection 0

2.

3.

1. Bespoke library shelves fully utilize the double-height living space and create an inviting area for relaxation. But the eye is still continually drawn to the outdoors.

2. The preserved structural trusses and steel I-beams form a dramatic framework over the newly carved-out urban garden, ensuring the building's industrial origins remain a key focus throughout the home.

3. The establishment of outdoor spaces within the original bare-brick warehouse walls was integral to the success of this award-winning project. Expansive glass doors offer continuous views and can be peeled back to connect the kitchen and outside deck, with its raised open-air pool. A kitchen island makes an effective connection with the pool and completes a remarkable summer entertaining space.

4. & **5**. Wire-brushed recycled eucalyptus wood was used throughout the property, both internally and on exterior facades. The versatile, tactile wood complements the raw materials of the warehouse and gains an attractive patina with age. With such careful attention to detailing, an old building not previously heritage listed is now considered a valued local landmark; upholding the neighbourhood's history.

'Our clients' brief was to "think creatively" and to preserve as much of the industrial character as possible while creating a light-filled home with a lush garden. The new courtyard garden is the heart of the design, but also effectively celebrates the heritage.'

ARCHITECT VIRGINIA KERRIDGE

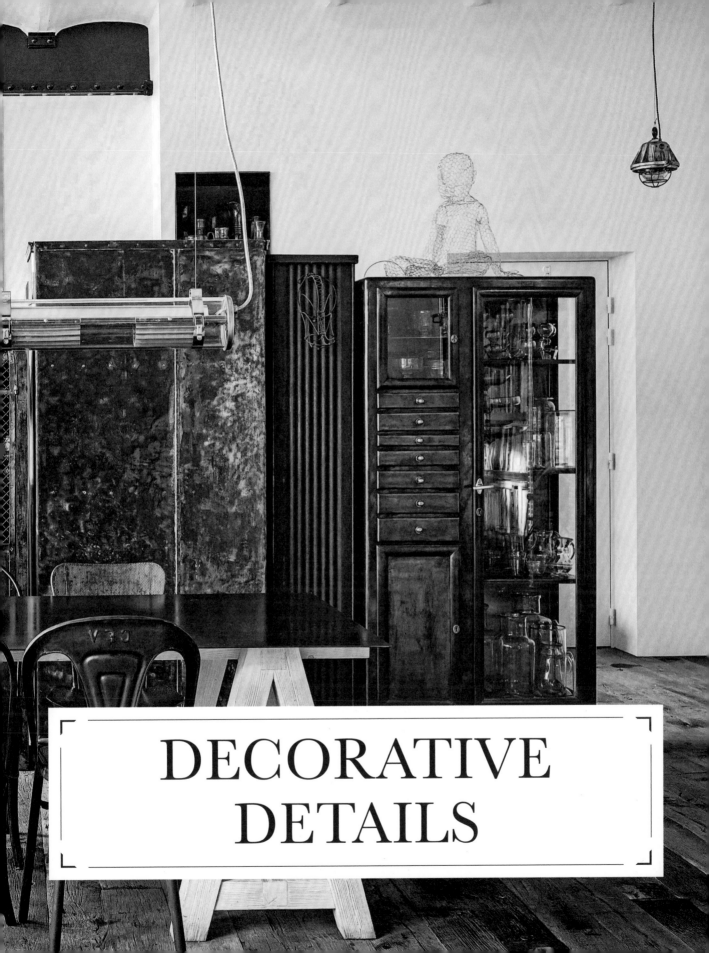

DECORATIVE
DETAILS

MATERIALS

Industrial buildings offer a distinctive backdrop for interior designers and homeowners with imagination and a sense of adventure. Original features such as exposed brickwork, raw concrete, original timbers and steel are often present and usually combined with heights and scales uncommon within more conventional homes. It is the juxtaposition of these authentic architectural attributes that presents exciting challenges and that makes factory and warehouse conversions truly remarkable residences. It is the decorative details, however, that complete a space. Old elements such as bricks and beams can be complemented by homeware designs that draw directly on their distinctive forms. Tactile materials like plywood are well-suited to industrial environs, while vintage industrial pieces and upcycled creations further enhance authentic structural features. Rough concrete surfaces can be counterbalanced by refined cement accessories. But the loft look and warehouse living can influence decor in any modern home. For those channelling industrial-style interiors, designers around the world are turning heavy-duty components into inventive pieces for the home.

◄◄ A converted factory in Milan comprises the offices and home of renowned architect Paula Navone. On the mezzanine, an aluminium 1930s military aviation cabinet doubles as a desk. The unit reflects the building's steel beams and is paired with a chic NICOLLE stool.

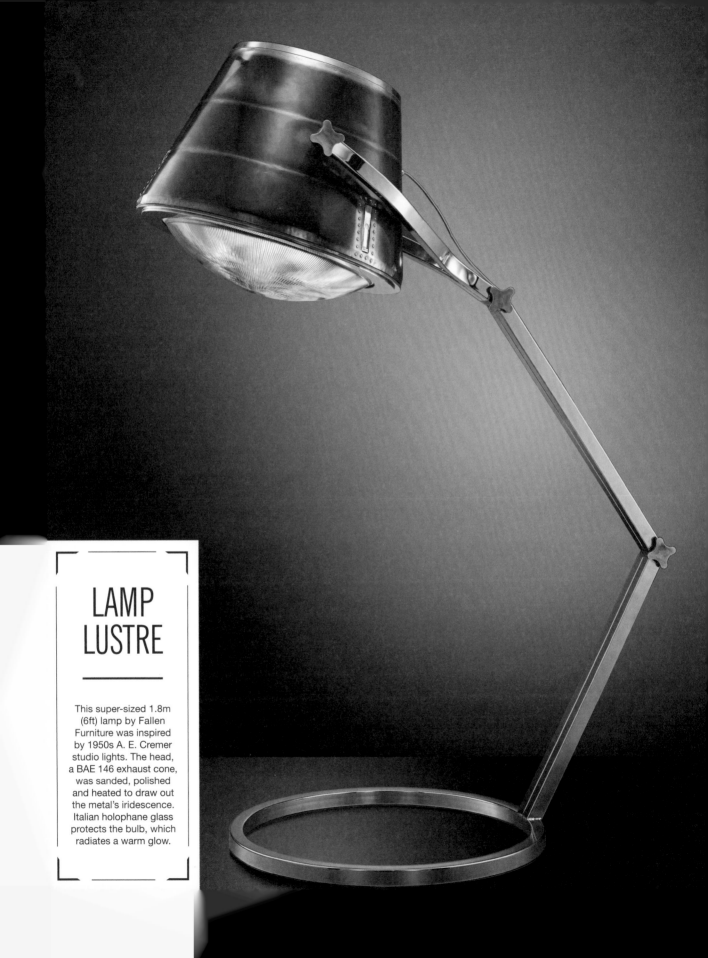

LAMP LUSTRE

This super-sized 1.8m (6ft) lamp by Fallen Furniture was inspired by 1950s A. E. Cremer studio lights. The head, a BAE 146 exhaust cone, was sanded, polished and heated to draw out the metal's iridescence. Italian holophane glass protects the bulb, which radiates a warm glow.

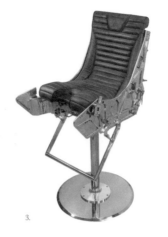

AVIATION

After years circling the globe, retired aeroplane machinery and materials are clocking up new mileage in interior design. Retired military planes and commercial airliners, remarkable feats of engineering, are being expertly upcycled and transformed into striking furniture and lighting for the home. Highly-polished aluminium and heavy-duty rivet details characterize these high-end aeronautical creations. These designs will really go the distance.

1. A huge fan from a Rolls-Royce Harrier Jump Jet forms the base of this stunning table by Intrepid Design. A glass top ensures every detail can be enjoyed during dinner. **2**. A section of Boeing 737 fuselage with windows finds new purpose as a room divider, created by California-based MotoArt. **3**. The renowned Mk10 ejection seat is estimated to have saved over 800 lives. In the hands of expert upcyclers Brett and Shane Armstrong of Hangar 54, decommissioned seats are converted into bar stools. **4**. This sizeable Aero wall clock by British designer Paul Firbank, The Rag and Bone Man, was fashioned from a Pratt & Whitney JT8 motor ring and finished with hands made from engine fan parts. **5**. It took six months for Bath-based firm Fallen Furniture to transform an RAF cluster bomb into this 2.4m-tall (8ft) liquor cabinet, The Bomb.

BEAMS

The I- or H-beam, also known as the Double-T, is a structural aluminium or steel beam with an I or H-shaped cross section. These beams bear very heavy loads in building construction and are often exposed in warehouse conversions to enhance the industrial aesthetic, but the iconic form has also inspired original interior accessories.

1.

2.

3.

4.

1. British designer Matthew Hilton honours a functional form with the I-Beam side table in American black walnut. **2**. The distinctly industrial Beam Chandelier by American lighting studio Luke Lamp Co combines steel, loops of flax rope and filament bulbs. **3**. Brooklyn-based Katch I.D. drew inspiration from the ubiquitous steel of New York's subway for their Supreme Beam design, transforming a heavy-duty shape into light-hearted bookends powder-coated in seven different colours. **4**. Glas Italia handcrafts glass furniture in the town of Macherio near Milan, Italy. This modern chaise longue comprises three slabs of smoked glass. **5**. Berlin-based furniture designers EAJY based their Beams chair on the construction of San Francisco's iconic Golden Gate Bridge. The chair's ash frame evidences the subtle influence of the I-beam form.

5.

1.

2.

British design studio StolenForm immortalized the classic London brick form as an imaginative ceramic vase and matching dish, which can be used to hold kitchen utensils or stationery. The brick vases can be stacked in a quirky display.

3.

BRICKS & BREEZE BLOCKS

Whether your home boasts its original exposed brickwork or you simply wish to channel the raw industrial aesthetic, these ingenious brick-based designs will complement any interior scheme.

1. The distinctive London brick was created in 1877. Billions have since been made and are still being produced. The iconic 'frogged' (indented) shape is recognizable the world over. In 2014, British designer Tom Dixon put the London brick to surprising use as a fragrance diffuser, pairing porous bricks with an original scent blended to evoke London's cityscape. **2.** This sturdy lamp by Unique's Co. features a brick base, copper piping neck and vintage-style valve. **3.** A brick installation dominates a wall in the Moscow loft of Natalia Onufreichuk, producer and stylist at *Architectural Digest Russia*. Each pre-revolution brick has a different manufacturer's stamp. **4.** Brooklyn-based interiors studio The New Design Project used cinder blocks to make a simple yet stylish bedside unit. It is easily reconfigured and spaces within the blocks are ideal for storage.

1.

2.

3.

4.

5.

6.

CAR PARTS

Beaten, bolted, welded and even stitched together, reclaimed car parts can take on an entirely new identity in the home. From accessories to larger items of furniture, including seating, these surprisingly refined creations are not just for petrolheads. Freewheel with the latest trend in interiors and test-drive this collection of quirky automotive designs.

1. The iconic curves of the VW Beetle have been transformed into this brilliant club chair and footstool by designer Paul Firbank, The Rag And Bone Man. 2. German studio Unibro Design specialize in upcycling automotive materials. This BMW Alpina boot sits on adjustable aluminium legs. 3. Retyred Furniture in New Zealand create durable homewares, including tables and chairs, from old tyres, rescuing them from landfill. 4. This colourful, tactile cushion by London-based design firm Ting has been imaginatively crafted from reclaimed seatbelts. 5. Racing Gold take the unseen parts of retired Formula One cars and craft striking pieces like this lamp, consisting of Red Bull gearbox pieces polished to a high shine. 6. Tinman Studio in Israel preserves car parts' scratches and original paintwork to create characterful furniture, including cabinets.

DESK CLAMP

In 1921, Bernard-Albin Gras designed a series of robust lamps for offices and industrial environments. The 211-311 table lamp for La Lampe Gras has a clamp base that fixes securely to a desktop, maximizing space and providing strong, focused light by which to work.

CLAMPS

A workshop staple, C- and G-shaped clamps are used to secure materials to a bench during construction. But the classic form is also now inspiring designers around the world to create quirky and clever homeware that can be moved with the twist of a screw.

1. The imaginatively named Spike–The Wild Bunch wall shelf was conceived by Konstantin Grcic for Italian brand Magis and is available from modern furniture site Made In Design. **2.** These colourful circular shelves from Stockholm-based Navet are an ideal way to add extra storage space. **3.** The aluminium Adjustable Clampersand from Hand-Eye Supply in Portland serves as a stylish bookend and channels the enduring industrial and typographic interiors trends. **4.** Frequently moving between different cities, designers Kyle Hoff and Alex O'Dell were inspired to create their steel Floyd legs, manufactured in Detroit, which can be clamped to different materials to create functional modular tables. **5.** This pretty candleholder from Aparentment fixes to the edge of tables or windowsills and can be used individually or as part of a quirky grouping.

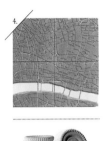

CONCRETE

Designers worldwide are demonstrating the versatility of concrete, making it easier than ever to inject an industrial edge into interiors. Raw concrete has become refined: cast and sculpted, polished smooth, etched with delicate details. These are design heavy-weights.

1. These concrete stools by Chinese studio Bentu have detachable legs and can be stacked up as shelves. **2**. The Heavy Pendant lights by Decode London prove that concrete can be used in unconventional contexts. **3**. Swedish brand SRF Hantverk has made brushes for over a century, employing visually impaired craftsmen, who make them by hand. This badger-hair brush fits neatly atop a concrete shaving cup. **4**. Greek designers A Future Perfect etch city maps into their Fragments coasters. **5**. Kast Concrete Knobs created this design for the debut issue of *Warehouse Home* magazine. It is named after Rosie The Riveter. **6**. The Tidvis grandfather clock by Johan Forsberg takes a strikingly contemporary form. **7**. The WEIGHT Vase by SPÉCIMEN Editions complements delicate flowers. **8**. Kast Concrete Basins bring industrial chic to a bathroom. **9**. Lyon Beton's Hauteville Armchair at Pad Home is a classic.

CRATES & CONTAINERS

Packing crates and shipping containers that once travelled the globe are being repurposed worldwide, and their functional forms are inspiring creative new designs too. From small side cabinets to more substantial storage, in a range of colours and finishes, this feel for freight is infectious. Modular and multi-purpose, this distinctive cargo-derived furniture will suit any space and is as stylish and funky as it is solid and functional.

2.

Handcrafted in India from sections of decommissioned shipping containers, these clever, colourful cabinets bear their original freight logos and signs of life on the high seas.

1.

3.
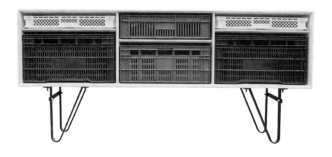

4.

1. This limited-edition wall-mounted drinks cabinet was once a military ammunition crate. With plenty of space for liquor, it is guaranteed to kick off any party with a bang. **2**. Kontainr Series Cabinets from Reason Season Time are fashioned from parts of decommissioned shipping containers. **3**. Architect and designer Mauricio Arruda uses recycled plastic crates as colourful drawers in furniture inspired by Brazil's local fruit and vegetable markets. **4**. These modular cabinets, based on freight containers, are made in the Netherlands. Available in any colour in the RAL range, stackable, and mounted on wheels, they can be customized to suit any unique scheme. **5**. The charming 'Sending Animals' storage range from Italian brand Seletti puts an irreverent twist on wooden packing crates to create fun and surprisingly practical furniture.

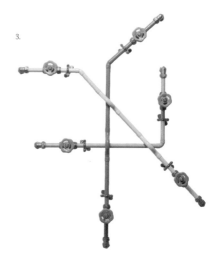

GALVANIZED PIPING

In many industrial buildings, surface-mounted galvanized piping on solid walls and ceilings conceals cabling and can be readily relocated or modified. It is a feature that lends a space a strong and stylish utilitarian aesthetic. A similar effect can be achieved in any home with these clever piping creations. A matt zinc finish contrasts well with wood and copper, although colour powder-coating is also achievable.

1. This galvanized steel-pipe bed frame was constructed exclusively for the launch issue of *Warehouse Home* magazine by Manchester-based design studio Urban Grain. Dressing the bed with pink and grey bed linens achieved an attractive soft industrial look. **2.** Lighting designer Tony Miles handmakes a range of distinctive table lamps formed from bent steel tubing. The Question Mark tall table lamp was sold through online store Rockett St George. **3.** British maker Nick Fraser produces functional interior products that blend charm, character and colour. This coat rack incorporates vintage-style faucets as 'hooks' and is available in various configurations. **4.** American home furnishings company Restoration Hardware offers this industrial pipe desk with shelving as a hard-working solution for any study.

4.

1.

2.

5.

3.

4.

6.

LOCKERS

Vintage factory or school lockers are spacious and sensible storage solutions. They add an authentic industrial feel to a residence and are even more characterful when still displaying the dents and scuffs of age and frequent use. The practical locker form, with its distinctive venting, is also influencing a new generation of imaginative designs.

1. These vintage industrial lockers date from the 1950s and were sourced from an old factory in Holland by British salvage expert Sean Cox. **2.** Brightly-coloured cabinets from Italian design house Seletti channel combination-lock details and typical locker features. **3.** This nine-door Copper Blush cabinet is available from Out There Interiors. It will add a sophisticated, soft industrial look to any space. **4.** Formed from sheet metal, powder-coated in a number of contemporary colours, the conventional metal cabinet has been restyled by Fratelli Lamière for modern living. **5.** The double-door B2 cabinet is manufactured by iconic French brand Tolix, in the same factory as their classic designs. **6.** The solid oak locky2 by Dutch designer Stephan Siepermann is a clever reinterpretation of archetypal sports lockers, complete with wooden padlock.

WOOD WORKS

This wooden armchair is part of the furniture series 'Les Palettes' by French designers Martin Leveque and Mathieu Maingourd. The range also includes a lounger, shelves and tables and a manual is available for those keen to undertake an upcycled furniture project themselves.

PALLETS

A staple of builders' yards and for the haulage industry, roughly hewn wooden pallets bear heavy loads and weather most conditions. But, off the fork-lift, hard-wearing pallets are being given a new lease of life as fun, serviceable furniture. Designers are also drawing inspiration from the slatted pallet shape. And while some re-work the basic form, other creations are surprisingly refined.

2.

1.

3.

4.

1. Artist Gavin Turk customized this Studiomama chair as part of a fundraising initiative for Argentine charity Amistad O Nada. **2.** Berlin-based designer Daniel Becker conceived the '45' series for furniture start-up Kimidori. Rather than working with pallets as constructed objects, he designed a cabinet, sideboard and seating made from their pine planks. Even after heavy sanding, years of use are still reflected in the wood and visible when the timber is set in geometric patterns at 45 and 90 degrees. **3.** These unusual pallet-wood light shades by British designer-maker Christopher Berry are available in five vibrant colours. **4.** London industrial design studio Plant & Moss combined traditional techniques and contemporary trends to craft this quirky coffee table. The 'pallets' can be used individually or stacked and are available in oak or walnut.

1.

PAPER

The tactile quality of recycled-paper designs makes them a stylish as well as sustainable decorative option. At *Warehouse Home*, we are passionate about reclaimed materials and supporting talented designer-makers. We ensure damaged copies of our magazine are imaginatively repurposed and will always promote striking paper-based homeware.

1. Dutch designer Debbie Wijskamp creates vases, bowls and other elegant decorative objects using recycled paper. 2. Each of the designs shown on this page was commissioned by *Warehouse Home* magazine and then created using damaged copies of the magazine. Becky Creed layered and bonded together dozens of sheets from the first issue to create a solid block, which was then turned on a lathe to create limited-edition pendant lights. 3. Wall and table clocks were crafted from pulped and dyed paper by BLURECO. 4. Processed paper 'beads' adorn the legs of an oak coffee table (left) by German designer Pia Wüstenberg. The Pulp stool (right) by Polish designer Paula Szwedkowicz incorporates a concrete-like pulp seat. 5., 6. and 7. The Quartz pulp lamp by Crea-re, Shredded Vase by Magie Hollingworth and set of layered vessels by Dan Hoolahan all started life as pages of Issue Three.

1.

2.

3.

PLYWOOD

Light-hued plywood has a distinctive strength and durability, as well as texture and warmth, making it a firm favourite with designers. A sustainable material, it has inspired playful and practical designs for decades. Unadorned or with a colourful twist, there is no question that veneer will go far.

4.

5.

6.

7.

1. The iconic Penguin Donkey by Egon Riss was first produced by Isokon Plus in 1939 and is still manufactured today. **2.** British designer Alex Swain channelled a love of typography and natural materials in the modernist ByALEX A Desk. This blue edition was designed exclusively for *Warehouse Home*. **3.** The simple form of the SB01-1 chair by British duo Baines & Fricker was inspired by a silhouette in a poster for the 1935 Zurich exhibition *Der Stuhl*. **4.** Swiss designer Nikki Kreis collaborated with *Warehouse Home* on this practical pegboard. **5.** The Loop table by Barber & Osgerby for Isokon Plus is a design classic. **6.** WEAMO create plywood accessories, including these colourful bookends. **7.** This Latvian birch plywood egg cup is by Kreisdesign. **8.** Japanese studio Drill Design create Paper-Wood stools by layering wood veneer and recycled paper in order to recreate the distinctive look of plywood.

DESIGN RULES

The impressive Printed Rulers wallpaper was designed by Mr & Mrs Vintage, the founders of leading wallpaper manufacturer NLXL. The high quality of the printing means every typographic detail can be enjoyed. Online suppliers include NLXL and The Orchard.

RULERS

From furniture finished with vintage yardsticks to handmade homeware and decorative prints, rulers are inching into every aspect of interior decor and adding a quirky twist to spaces large and small. Whether metric or imperial, vintage originals or modern makings, ruler-based designs certainly measure up.

1. London-based designer Rory Dobner has fulfilled a variety of prestigious interior design briefs all around the world and his original work includes an ever-expanding homeware collection. Dobner repurposed old vintage rulers to craft this imaginative pendant light shade. **2**. This yardstick clock, the creation of Southern Inspired Arts, would make a very eye-catching addition to any wall. **3**. Industrial steel-framed tables are hand made to order in a number of sizes for London antiques and retro store The Old Cinema. Their tabletops are inlaid with individually sourced, vintage wooden yardsticks. **4**. This characterful coat rack from The Old Cinema is crafted from American yardsticks of various ages and origins. **5**. These limited-edition waste-paper bins, featured on Not On The High Street, are made from reclaimed wooden school rulers.

1.

2.

4.

3.

STEEL DRUMS

Once used to ship liquids and powders, steel cargo barrels are barely recognizable when reimagined as furniture and lighting. Sliced into sections, cut into squares, some designs retain the drums' original patina; others are polished to a high shine or repainted. This is quirky, eco-conscious decor.

5.

6.

7.

1. Petal Chairs are made in small independent workshops in Albania for PO! Paris. **2**. The Palette Cabinet is a colourful upcycling creation by Italian designers Vibrazioni Art-Design. **3**. French artisans Dentelles Et Bidons cut fretwork-like patterns into drums, which are then powder-coated. This oversized lamp is ideal for balconies or gardens. **4**. Lichtfass Company hand-select steel barrels for their dents, rustiness and distinctive tones and slice them to form giant pendant shades. **5**. Salvaged steel triangles were welded together to form this origami-style side table from The Old Cinema. **6**. This Phillips Collection Oil Drum Mirror retains its authentic paint and patina. **7**. American upcycler Wes Bennett transformed a steel drum into the unique DOT circular bookshelf. **8**. This unique Cafe Chair is another clever creation by Vibrazioni, made from steel drums cut and welded almost entirely by hand.

8.

1.

VINTAGE LINEN

Woven from flax, hemp or jute, tactile and durable burlap is ideal for upholstery. In the hands of talented designers, humble 'gunny sacks', previously used for coffee beans and rice, are remade as attractive accessories and furnishings. Hessian fabric's heritage appearance suits any industrial interior and stencilled monograms add to its character.

2.

3.

4.

5.

1. Lucy Curtis, founder of Corset Laced Mannequins, individually selects fabrics to cover and modify old mannequins. Vintage hessian, such as this French flour sacking, gives a finished mannequin a delightful historical appearance. **2**. British upcycler Ursh Stevens of Refunk'd created these quirky pendant shades from reclaimed sacking with colourful, stencilled lettering. **3**. A coffee-bean sack cushion from Mipo is a charming addition to any seat or sofa. Oversized buttons add to its character. **4**. Irish designer Kelly Swallow upholstered this antique Wing chair in rare German grain sacks. Dating from 1924, the herringbone linen sacks were once used on family farms and feature elaborate motifs and smart blue woven stripes. **5**. Coffee bean sacks were used to create these beanbag cubes from Gus Modern; they make ideal footstools and are just as fun whether displayed individually or in a set.

ICONIC DESIGNS

The dramatic growth in manufacturing that occurred during the Industrial Revolution resulted in exciting innovations in furniture and lighting design. As factory work became more specialized, production lines faster, new devices and systems were conceived to improve the safety and comfort of the workforce. Adjustable lamps provided focused light on workspaces and small mechanisms. Ergonomic chairs were developed, with sculpted backrests and pivoting frames. Stackable furniture offered a space-saving solution. Expertly engineered, the quality and functionality of the creations established new standards in design; they became benchmarks for other products. It was only a matter of time before they would make a transition from the factory floor to homes. Groundbreaking for their time, the robust industrial designs of the early twentieth century have also proved timeless. They have inspired generations of architects and designers and informed many contemporary practices and applications. Often emulated and even copied, these iconic originals cannot be matched. These intelligent and imaginative designs have a revered place in history and a certain future.

◄ NICOLLE stools and chairs were conceived in France in 1933 in order to match the latest health and safety standards for factories and workshops. The resilient yet comfortable construction ensured the seats were widely adopted for use in textile and mechanical plants.

EVOLUTION OF DESIGNS

Innovative in their own time, each of these iconic brands still survives today. While some still cater specifically to industrial requirements, many old brands have transitioned from warehouse to home.

1851
Smiths

Founded in 1851, Smiths became the largest clock manufacturer in Europe, producing clocks for the motor industry, aircraft, railway stations and the home. Roger Lascelles in London today have the exclusive trademarks to produce Smiths designs.

1893
Slingsby

Harry Crowther Slingsby first obtained orders for labour-saving trolleys in 1893. A patent was filed the following year for the Slingsby Sliding Wheel Truck. By 1901, Slingsby owned the largest truck shop in the world. It now offers 35,000 products.

1898
Holophane

Holophane has produced lighting solutions from its UK-based facility for over 120 years and the name has become synonymous with quality luminaires. Holophane's innovative prismatic glass refractors and reflectors improve the ability to control light.

1921
Lampe Gras

In 1921, Bernard-Albin Gras designed a series of task lamps for offices and industrial settings. Sturdy and ergonomic, the Gras lamps were immediately popular with architect Le Corbusier, who used the lighting on his own desk and in projects globally.

RIGHT
ANGLE

A pioneering balance
system, using special
springs under constant
tension, was developed
in 1931 by automotive
engineer, George
Carwardine. A patent
was filed. The first four-
spring Anglepoise task
lamp launched in 1933.
A three-spring version
soon followed for homes.

1934

Tolix; Standard Chair

The entrepreneur Xavier Pauchard used galvanized sheet-metal to produce robust, stackable Tolix chairs. In the same year, the new Standard Chair was invented by engineer, architect and designer Jean Prouvé. Its wide back legs support the weight of the user. It is crafted in compressed sheet metal.

1933

Coolicon; Anglepoise; Chaises NICOLLE

The NICOLLE chair, with its whale-tail-shaped backrest and distinctive swan neck is still made in France, using the very same techniques and tools as the original. The Coolicon high-gloss, enamel-coated shade has lit factories, mills, hospitals and the London Underground. A classic relaunched for production in Britain.

1950

Jieldé

Jieldé lamps take their name from the initials of inventor Jean-Louis Domecq. Their simple yet sturdy form, based on an articulating arm, made the lamps very popular in workshops and factories. By the 1990s, they were entering homes as well. They are still handmade in Lyon, using the original equipment.

1944

Emeco

The original 1006 Navy chair was created for the American Navy. The Electrical Machine and Equipment Company (Emeco) in Pennsylvania conceived 77 steps to transform ordinary recycled aluminium, in plentiful supply, into exceptionally strong aluminium for the high seas. The estimated lifespan is 150 years.

IMAGE CREDITS

Front Cover Styling by Jemima Heatherington, photography by Rory Gardiner **2–3** Bruce Damonte **6** LatitudeStock/Alamy Stock Photo **9** Jaime Alvarez **10–11** Jean Allsopp **12** Joe Fletcher **14** Bruce Damonte **15** Richard Barnes **16–17** Sharon Risedorph **18–19** Colleen Duffley **20–21** Production Laurence Dougier, photography Nicolas Mathéus **22** Mark Roskams **23** Chuck Choi **24–25** Jordi Miralles **26–29** Luc Roymans **30** Frank Oudeman **32–33** Eduard Hueber **34** Simon Feneley **35** Jim Stephenson **36–37** Seth Caplan **38** Lincoln Barbour **39** *Top* Jordi Miralles *Bottom* Peter Landers **40–41** Peter Landers **42–47** Production Tami Christiansen, photography Nathalie Krag **48** Catherine Tighe **50–53** Kat Alves **54–55** Laurent Saint Jean **56** *Top* Photography Photoplan, courtesy of Urban Spaces *Bottom* Photography Luke White, courtesy of The Interior Archive **57** Photography Photoplan, courtesy of Urban Spaces **58** Nicolas Mathéus **59** Catherine Tighe **60–61** Castle+Beatty **62–63** French+Tye **64–71** Shannon McGrath **72** Max Zambelli **73** Production Helle Walsted, photography wichmann+bendtsen **74–75** Production Helle Walsted, photography wichmann+bendtsen **76** Max Zambelli **77, 78** Production Helle Walsted, photography wichmann+bendtsen **79** *Left* Max Zambelli *Right* Production Helle Walsted, Photography wichmann+bendtsen **80** Jean Luc Laloux **82** Costas Picadas, courtesy of GAP Photos **83** Photo by Ben Hoffmann/Contour by Getty Images **84** Jean Luc Laloux **85** © Paul Massey/Livingetc/Time Inc UK **86–87** Jean Allsopp **88–91** Kristofer Johnsson **92–93** Jason Lindberg **94–95** Peter Landers **96–103** Jesper Ray **104–9** Gaelle Le Boulicaut **110** Black & Steil **111–14** Ball & Albanese **115** Black & Steil **116** Ball & Albanese **117** *Left* Black & Steil *Right* Ball & Albanese **118** Photo by Ben Hoffmann/Contour by Getty Images **120–21** Jonathan Maloney **122** Jim Stephenson **123** Jordi Miralles **124** Emily Andrews **125** *Top* Emily Andrews *Bottom* Jim Stephenson **126** Bruce Damonte **127** Carl Wooley **128–29** Ruben Ortiz **130–31** Beppe Brancato **132** Stephen Clement **133** *Top* Ben Hosking *Bottom* Joy von Tiedemann **134–38** Lluis Carbonell **139** Richard Powers **140** Lluis Carbonell **141** Richard Powers **142** Ed Reeve **144–45** Donna Griffith, courtesy of *Covet Garden* **146–47** Tim Williams **148** Stephen Clement **149** Albert Vecerka, courtesy of Esto **150–51** Derek Swalwell **152** Csaba Barbay **153** Valentino Bellini **154–59** Ed Reeve **160** Styling Daniel Rozensztroch, photography Jerome Galland, courtesy of and copyright Marie Claire Maison **162–63** Andrew Beasley **164–65** Paul Dyer **166** Michael Moran, courtesy of OTTO **167** Paul Craig **168** Stephen Clement **169** Birgitta Wolfgang, courtesy of Sisters Agency **170–71** Scott Amundson **172–73** Alberta+Mia Dominguez **174–79** David Lauer **180–87** Production Tami Christiansen, photography Nathalie Krag, courtesy of Taverne Agency **188** Rory Gardiner **190–93** Csaba Barbay **194–95** Derek Swalwell **196–97** Dash Marshall **198–203** Oliver Perrott **204–211** Rory Gardiner **212** Photography Jean-Marc Wullschleger, courtesy of Living Agency **214–15** Rien van Rijthoven **216** Honestone **217** Fraser Marsden **218–19** Peter Landers **220** Tom Ferguson **221** Luuk Kramer **222–25** Alexander James **226** Birgitta Wolfgang, courtesy of Sisters Agency **228–29** Filip Dujardin **230–31** Toshiyuki Yano **232** Marc van Praag **233** Photo by Ben Hoffmann/Contour by Getty Images **234–41** Frank Oudeman **242–47** Styling by Jemima Heatherington, photography Rory Gardiner **248** Peter Kooijman **250–51** Shannon McGrath **252–53** Steve Back **254–55** Tom Ferguson **256–57** Shannon McGrath **258–59** Debbie Bragg **260–61** Gaelle Le Boulicaut **262–63** Peter Kooijman **264–69** Albert Vecerka, courtesy of Esto **270–73** Michael Nicholson **274–75** Styling Daniel Rozensztroch, photography Jerome Galland, courtesy of and copyright Marie Claire Maison **276** Enrico Conti **279** Aero Clock by The Rag and Bone Man, photography Damian Griffiths **280** I-Beam Side Table by Matthew Hilton, courtesy of De La Espada; Beam Chandelier by Luke Lamp Co, photography Luke Kelly; Supreme Beam by Katch I.D., photography Jason Hamilton; I-Beam lounge chair by Glas Italia, courtesy of Made In Design **282** Scent Collector Diffuser, courtesy of Tom Dixon; Industrial London Brick Lamp by Unique's Co., courtesy of notonthehighstreet.com; Brick Dish and Brick Vase by StolenForm, photography Jack Greenwood; apartment of Natalia Onufreichuk, Producer and Interior Stylist at *AD Russia* magazine, and Dmitriy Telkov, photography Sergey Ananiev **283** Upper East Side Apartment by The New Design Project, photography Alan Gastelum **284** Beetle Bonnett Club Chair with Bootlid Footstool by The Rag and Bone Man, photography Damian Griffiths; **285** Red Bull Racing F1 Small Gear Lamp by Racing Gold, photography Thomas Butler/Realise Creative; Toyota Cabinet by Ronen Wasserman, Tinman Studio, photography Keith Glassman **286** Lampe Gras N°211-311, photography Ian Scigliuzzi, courtesy of François Muracciole and DCW Éditions **287** Wild Bunch Shelf by Magis, courtesy of Made In Design; Clamp Trays by Navet, photography Viktor Sjödin, copyright Navet; Clamp Candle, photography seen.me **289** Decode London Heavy Pendant Lights, courtesy of Made In Design; Kast Concrete Knobs, photography Grey Hensey; Weight Vase Model B by SPÉCIMEN Editions, courtesy of Made In Design; Concrete Basin, courtesy of Kast Concrete Basins; Hauteville Armchair by Lyon Beton, courtesy of Pad Home **290** Bomb Bar by Oliver Apt, photography Ilia Bizi; José Collection by Mauricio Arruda Design, photography Felipe Moroni; Pandora Cabinet, courtesy of Sander Mulder **292** Soft industrial bedroom scheme for Warehouse Home Issue One, styled by Sophie Bush and Carole Poirot, photography Charlie Surbey; Industrial Tube Pipe Tap Table Lamp by Tony Miles, © Rockett St George, photography Jane Rockett; Pipework Coat Rack Edition by Nick Fraser, photography James Champion **293** Industrial Pipe Desk by Restoration Hardware © 2014 RH **294** Vintage lockers, photography Sean Cox, courtesy of Turner & Cox **295** Ronzinante Locker by Fratelli Lamière, photography Sara Anfossi; locky2 by Stephan Siepermann, photography Stephan Siepermann **296** Charles Edouard Armchair by M&M Designers, photography Jérôme Blin **297** Pallet Chair by Studiomama, photography Gavin Turk; Pallet Pendant Shade by Christopher Berry, Factory Twenty One, photography Nicola Kirk **298** Debbie Wijskamp for Serax, courtesy of Serax maison d'être **299** Turned Paper Light by Becky Creed, photography Darryl Crowley; all other items photographed by Oliver Perrott **300** Penguin Donkey by Isokon Plus, courtesy of Skandium; A Desk for Warehouse Home by ByALEX, photography Sun Lee; SB01-1 Chair by Baines & Fricker, photography Yeshen Venema; Plywood pegboard by Kreisdesign, photography Sun Lee; Loop Table by Isokon Plus, courtesy of Skandium; Streamline Original Bookend by WEAMO, photography Richard Wearmouth; Plywood Egg Cup by Kreisdesign, photography Nikki Kreis **301** Paper-Wood Stool by Drill Design, photography Takumi Ota **302** Printed Rulers wallpaper by Mr & Mrs Vintage for NLXL Lab, courtesy of Pad Home **303** Yardstick Clock by Lisa Henderson, Southern Inspired Arts, photography Laurie Slagle; American Yardstick Table and Coat Rack, courtesy of The Old Cinema; School Ruler Waste-Paper Bins, courtesy of notonthehighstreet.com **304** Petal Chair by PO! Paris, photography narophoto.com; Palette Cabinet by Vibrazioni, photography Callo Albanese; Steel Drum Lamp by Dentelles Et Bidons, photography Vincent Guilbaud; Salvaged Steel Stool, courtesy of The Old Cinema; DOT circular bookshelf, courtesy of Wes Bennett **305** Cafe Chair by Vibrazioni, photography Callo Albanese **307** Vintage Grain Sack Pendant Lampshades by Refunk'd and Vintage Grain Sack Cushion by Mipo, photography Jack Greenwood; Antique Wing Chair by Kelly Swallow, photography Michael Swallow **308** NICOLLE SARL **310** Slingsby trolley, courtesy of Slingsby; Vintage Holophane Pendant Light, courtesy of LASSCO **311** Anglepoise Type 75 Lamps, photography Jake Curtis **312** Nicolle chair, photography Patrice Pascal; A Chair, courtesy of Tolix; Standard Chair, courtesy of Vitra **313** Navy Chair by Emeco, courtesy of The Conran Shop; Jieldé Lamp, courtesy of Holloways of Ludlow **314** François Muracciole, photography Marie-Pierre Morel **319** Oliver Perrott

ARCHITECTS

A+Z Design, a-z.eu.com (Riverloft, Budapest; Loft 19, Budapest)
AABE, aabe.be (Warehouse Conversion, Düsseldorf)
adn architectures, a-dn.be (Loft FOR, Brussels)
Adrian Amore Architects, aaarchitects.com.au (Loft Apartment, Melbourne)
Airhouse Design Office, airhouse.jp (Warehouse, Yoro)
Allen Jack+Cottier, architectsajc.com (Inner City Warehouse, Sydney)
Alloy Development, alloyllc.com (185 Plymouth Street, New York)
ANDarchitects, andarchitects.com (Blesso Eco Warehouse, New York)
Andrew Franz Architect, andrewfranz.com (TriBeCa Loft, New York)
Andrew Simpson Architects, asimpson.com.au (Water Factory, Melbourne)
Anima, anima.cc (Rakovsky Loft, New York)
APA, apalondon.com (Residence Clerkenwell Apartment, London)
Architects EAT, eatas.com.au (Fitzroy Loft, Melbourne)
Axis Mundi Design, axismundi.com (Bond Street Loft, New York)
Bernadette Jacques, bernadette-jacques.be (Loft 65, Villefranche Sur Mer)
BG Architecture, bgarchitecture.com.au (Warehouse Conversion, Melbourne)
BK Interior Design, bkinteriordesign.com (Gentleman's Loft, New York)
BKA Architecture, bka.com.au (Paddington Warehouse, Sydney)
Bright Common Architecture & Design, brightcommon.com (The Pickle Factory, Philadelphia)
Castel Veciana Arquitectura, castelveciana.com (Loft Mialma, Barcelona)
CCS Architecture, ccs-architecture.com (Warehouse Conversion, San Francisco)
Cecconi Simone, cecconisimone.com (The Wrigley Loft, Toronto)
Charles Burkhalter, charlesburkhalter.com (Arne Svenson & Charles Burkhalter Residence, New York)
Chris Dyson Architects, chrisdyson.co.uk (The Cooperage, London; Shoreditch Warehouse, London)
Chris Hawley Architects, chrishawleyarchitects.com (Laundry Residence, Fargo)
Corben Architects, corben.com.au (Inner West Warehouse, Sydney)
Dash Marshall, dashmarshall.com (TriBeCa Loft, New York)
Delson or Sherman Architects PC, delsonsherman.com (Boerum Hill House, New York)
Design Initiative, design-initiative.net (Cheryl Morgan Loft, Birmingham Alabama)
Dow Jones Architects, dowjonesarchitects.com (Former Warehouse, London)
Edmonds + Lee Architects, edmondslee.com (The Oriental Warehouse, San Francisco)
Erica Severns Architect, ericaseverns.com (Hyde Garage, San Francisco)
Flow Works, flow.nu (Marius Haverkamp Residence, Amsterdam)
François Muracciole, fmuracciole.com (Anne Hubert Loft, Mulhouse; Faubourg-du-Temple Loft, Paris)
Frank&Faber and **Element-Studio**, formerly Trunk Creative, frankandfaber.co.uk, elementstudio.co.uk (Aeronautical Factory, London)
Gachot, gachotstudios.com (David Karp Loft, New York)
Garcia Tamjidi Architecture Design, garciatamjidi.com (Residence 3, San Francisco)
GRAUX & BAEYENS architecten, graux-baeyens.be (Binnenskamers, Kortrijk)
Gresford Architects, gresfordarchitects.co.uk (Paper Mill Studio, London)
Gumuchdjian Architects, gumuchdjian.com (Talisman Building, London)
HILLWORKS, hillworks.us (David Hill Residence, Auburn)
Inside Out Architecture, io-a.com (Clerkenwell Loft, London; Clerkenwell Loft Number 3, London; New Concordia Wharf, London)
Jackson Clements Burrows, jcba.com.au (The Golden Crust Bakery, Melbourne)
Jane Kim Design, janekimdesign.com (Franklin Street Loft, New York)

Jessica Helgerson Interior Design, jhinteriordesign.com (NW 13th Avenue Loft, Portland)
Joel Sanders Architect, joelsandersarchitect.com (Blesso Eco Warehouse, New York)
Katty Schiebeck, kattyschiebeck.com (Concrete Loft In Gracia, Barcelona)
Kurt Roessler Architect (Gentleman's Loft, New York)
LINEOFFICE Architecture, lineofficearchitecture.com (SOMA Loft, San Francisco)
Marco Vido, marcovido.com (Marco Vido Loft, Milan)
Mark Lewis Interior Design, marklewisinteriordesign.com (Hoxton Square Apartment, London)
Mass Operations, massoperations.com (Art Loft Chai Wan, Hong Kong)
Mei architects and planners, mei-arch.eu (Jobsveem Warehouse, Rotterdam)
Michael Haverland Architect, michaelhaverland.com (Industrial Conversion, New York)
Miriam Almanzar, miriamalmanzar.com (Loft Mialma, Barcelona)
Nia Morris Studio, niamorris.co.uk (The Old Aeroworks, London)
ODA New York, oda-architecture.com (Hubert Street, New York)
Paola Navone, paolanavone.it (Silkworm Factory, Spello)
Paolo Frello & Partners, frello.com (Loft Col Di Lana, Milan)
Pollard Thomas Edwards, pollardthomasedwards.co.uk (New Concordia Wharf, London)
Poteet Architects, poteetarchitects.com (Robison Loft, San Antonio)
Q-bic, q-bic.it (Pallets Loft, Florence)
Quintana Partners, quintanapartners.com (Loft Rflor, Barcelona)
Ricardo Bofill Taller de Arquitectura, ricardobofill.com (Cement Factory, Sant Just Desvern)
Robb Studio, robbstudio.com (Troyer Flour Mill Loft Condo, Denver)
Rochesters, rochesters.uk.com, (The Factory, London)
Ronald Janssen Architecten, ronaldjanssen.eu (Gearwheel Factory, Amsterdam)
Sadie Snelson Architects, ssarchitects.co.uk (Clapton Warehouse, London)
SchappacherWhite Architecture D.P.C., schappacherwhite.com (Hudson Loft, New York)
Sheep + Stone Interiors, sheepandstone.com, (DUMBO Warehouse, New York)
SheltonMindel, sheltonmindel.com (TriBeCa Industrial Loft, New York)
Slade Architecture, sladearch.com (Greene Street Loft, New York)
Stack London Ltd, stacklondon.co.uk (Paper Mill Studio, London)
Stanley Saitowitz | Natoma Architects Inc, saitowitz.com (McCarthy Loft, San Francisco)
Stephen Collins Interior Design, scid.com.au (Warehouse Conversion, Surry Hills)
Studio Gild, studiogild.com (Troyer Flour Mill Loft Condo, Denver)
Studio Kyson, kyson.co.uk (Scrutton Street, London)
Technē Architecture + Interior Design, techne.com.au (Regent Street Warehouse, Melbourne)
The Turett Collaborative, turettarch.com (Greenwich Street Loft, New York)
Virginia Kerridge Architect, vk.com.au (Lilyfield Warehouse, Sydney)
Wessel de Jonge Architecten BNA BV, wesseldejonge.nl (Jobsveem Warehouse, Rotterdam)
William Tozer Associates, williamtozerassociates.com (Horizontal House, London)
WILLIS+CO., willis-sf.com (Hyde Garage, San Francisco)

STOCKISTS

A Future Perfect, afutureperfect.gr
Anglepoise, anglepoise.com
Any Old Lights, anyoldlights.co.uk
Aparentment, aparentment.com
ARAM, aram.co.uk
Aria, ariashop.co.uk
Armac Martin, martin.co.uk
Aston Matthews,
    astonmatthews.co.uk
Bad Dog Designs,
    bad-dog-designs.co.uk
Baines&Fricker,
    bainesandfricker.net
Barber & Osgerby,
    barberosgerby.com
Becky Creed, beckycreed.co.uk
Benjamin Moore,
    benjaminmoore.com
Bentu, bentudesign.com
Blue Ticking, blueticking.co.uk
BLURECO, blureco.com
Buster + Punch,
    busterandpunch.com
ByALEX, byalex.co.uk
Cambrewood, cambrewood.com
Carl Hansen & Son, carlhansen.com
Carocim, carocim.com
Chaises Nicolle, chaises-nicolle.com
Clo20c, clo20c.com
Corset Laced Mannequins,
    corsetlacedmannequins.co.uk
Crea-re, crea-re.com
Crittall Windows,
    crittall-windows.co.uk
Daniel Becker Design Studio,
    danielbecker.eu
DCW Éditions, dcw-editions.fr
Debbie Wijskamp,
    debbiewijskamp.com
Decode London, decode.london
Dee Puddy, deepuddy.co.uk
De La Espada, delaespada.com
Dentelles & Bidons,
    dentellesetbidons.com
Dowsing & Reynolds,
    dowsingandreynolds.com
Drill Design, drill-design.com
Drummonds, drummonds-uk.com
Dyke & Dean, dykeanddean.com
EAJY, eajy.de
Emeco, emeco.net
Etsy, etsy.com
Factory 20, factory20.com

Factory Twenty One,
    factorytwentyone.co.uk
Fallen Furniture, fallenfurniture.com
Floyd Design LLC, floyddetroit.com
Forsberg Form, forsbergform.com
Frank Allart & Company,
    frankallart.com
Fritz Hansen, fritzhansen.com
George Smith, georgesmith.co.uk
Gervasoni, gervasoni1882.it
Glas Italia, glasitalia.com
GP Light & More,
    gplightandmore.com
Graham & Green,
    grahamandgreen.co.uk
Gus Modern, gusmodern.com
Hand-Eye Supply,
    handeyesupply.com
Hanger 54, hangar54.com
Heal's, heals.com
Holloways of Ludlow,
    hollowaysofludlow.com
Home Barn, homebarnshop.co.uk
IKEA, ikea.com
Intrepid Design,
    intrepid-design.co.uk
Iris Hantverk, irishantverk.se
Isokon Plus, isokonplus.com
Jieldé, jielde.com
Kast Concrete Basins,
    kastconcretebasins.com
Kast Concrete Knobs,
    lambornstudio.com
Katch Design, katchid.com
Kelly Swallow, kellyswallow.com
Knoll, knoll.com
Kreisdesign, kreisdesign.com
La Cerise sur le gâteau,
    lacerisesurlegateau.fr
Lamborn Studio,
    lambornstudio.com
LASSCO, lassco.co.uk
Lichtfass Company,
    lichtfasscompany.com
LINTELOO, linteloo.com
Loomlight, loomlightdesign.co.uk
Louis Poulsen, louispoulsen.com
Luke Lamp Co, lukelampco.com
Lyon Beton, lyon-beton.com
Made In Design,
    madeindesign.co.uk
Magie Hollingworth,
    magiehollingworth.co.uk

Magis, magisdesign.com
Martina Salvato, martinasalvato.com
Matthew Hilton, matthewhilton.com
Mauricio Arruda Design,
    mauricioarruda.net
Mayfly Vintage, mayflyvintage.co.uk
Merci, merci-merci.com
Michael Anastassiades,
    michaelanastassiades.com
Millington & Hope,
    millingtonandhope.com
Mipo, mipo.co.uk
MotoArt, motoart.com
NAVET, navetsthlm.com
Nest, nest.co.uk
Nick Fraser, nickfraser.co.uk
NLXL, nlxl.com
Not On The High Street,
    notonthehighstreet.com
Ochre, ochre.net
Oliver Apt, oliverapt.com
Out There Interiors,
    outthereinteriors.com
Owl and the Elephant,
    owlandtheelephant.co.uk
Pad Home, padhome.co.uk
Phillips Collection,
    phillipscollection.com
piadesign, piadesign.eu
Pipe Art, pipeart.co.uk
Plant & Moss, plantandmoss.com
PO! Paris, po-paris.com
Poliform, poliform.it
Prandina, prandina.it
Racing Gold, racinggold.co.uk
Reason Season Time,
    reasonseasontime.co.uk
Refunk'd, refunked.com
Restoration Hardware,
    restorationhardware.com
Retyred Furniture,
    retyredfurniture.co.nz
Rigg, rigg.uk
Robert Kime, robertkime.com
Rockett St George,
    rockettstgeorge.co.uk
Roll & Hill, rollandhill.com
Rory Dobner, rorydobner.com
Sander Mulder, sandermulder.com
Sara Ricciardi, sararicciardi.org
SCP, scp.co.uk
Seletti, seletti.com
Skandium, skandium.com

Skinflint, skinflintdesign.co.uk
Spécimen Editions,
    specimen-editions.fr
Steel Vintage, steelvintage.com
Stephan Siepermann,
    stephansiepermann.com
StolenForm, stolenform.com
Studiomama, studiomama.com
Sugden and Daughters,
    sugdenanddaughters.co.uk
The Conran Shop, conranshop.co.uk
The Den & Now,
    thedenandnow.com
The Gifted Few, thegiftedfew.com
The Light Yard, thelightyard.com
The Rag And Bone Man,
    theragandboneman.co.uk
The Old Cinema,
    theoldcinema.co.uk
The Old Yard, theoldyard.co.uk
The Orchard Home and Gifts,
    theorchardhomeandgifts.com
Timothy Oulton,
    timothyoulton.co.uk
Ting London, tinglondon.com
Tinman Studio, ronentinman.com
Tolix, tolix.fr
Tom Dixon, tomdixon.net
Trainspotters, trainspotters.co.uk
Turner & Cox, turnerandcox.co.uk
TwentyTwentyOne,
    twentytwentyone.com
Unibro Design, unibro.de
Unique's Co, uniquestr.com
Urban Grain, urbangrain.co.uk
USM Modular Furniture, usm.com
Utology, utology.co.uk
Vibrazioni Art Design,
    vibrazioniartdesign.com
Vincent and Barn,
    vincentandbarn.co.uk
Vintage Cushions,
    vintagecushions.com
Vintage Matters,
    vintagematters.co.uk
Vitsœ, vitsoe.com
Vitra, vitra.com
Warehouse Home Shop,
    mywarehousehome.com/shop
Water Monopoly,
    thewatermonopoly.com
WEAMO, weamofurniture.co.uk
XLCORK, xlcork.com

INDEX

WAREHOUSE HOME

Biannual Magazine
mywarehousehome.com/newspaper

Online Shop
mywarehousehome.com/shop

Interiors Blog
mywarehousehome.com

Design Service
yourhome@mywarehousehome.com

Social Media
mywarehousehome

From The Author: This book is dedicated to four special people, with far more gratitude and affection than I can articulate on paper: to my husband Oliver, my parents Peter and Beren, and to my brother Harry. My sincere thanks to Warehouse Home Art Editor Kate Ashton and our Creative Director Paul Rider, to Rachel Anderson, Mary Ormerod and the rest of the Warehouse Home team, and to all at Thames & Hudson who so enthusiastically supported the debut *Warehouse Home* book.

Front cover: Clapton Warehouse by Sadie Nelson Architects, London, UK (p. 242). Photographed by Rory Gardiner, rory-gardiner.com
Back cover, left: Upholstery Factory by Mark Lewis Interior Design, London, UK (p. 208). Photographed by Rory Gardiner, rory-gardiner.com
Back cover, right: Flour Mill by Studio Gild and Robb Studio, Denver, USA (p. 174). Photographed by David Lauer, davidlauerphotography.com
pp. 2–3: Oriental Warehouse by Edmonds + Lee Architects, San Francisco, USA. Photographed by Bruce Damonte, brucedamonte.com
pp. 10–11: Architect and architectural professor Cheryl Morgan resides in this converted warehouse in Birmingham, Alabama, characterized by raw brickwork and towering columns. Enormous windows ensure a seamless connection between the open-plan interior and courtyard.
pp. 274–75: In the home of Daniel Rozensztroch, creative director of Merci, a wall of vintage metal lockers creates an effective partition between the kitchen and living room. The table, comprising a metal plate on wooden trestles, was designed by Paola Navone for Gervasoni.
p. 314: Photographer Marie-Pierre Morel enlisted architect François Muracciole to transform this old metal workshop in Faubourg-du-Temple, Paris, into her home. He selected raw materials to complement the building's authentic features, such as scrap iron for the mezzanine library.
Line illustrations by Paul Rider, Creative Director of Warehouse Home.

First published in the United Kingdom in 2017 by Thames & Hudson Ltd, 181A High Holborn, London WC1V 7QX

Reprinted 2019

Warehouse Home: Industrial Inspiration for Twenty-First-Century Living © 2017 Sophie Bush

British Library Cataloguing-in-Publication Data
A catalogue record for this book is available from the British Library

ISBN 978-0-500-51946-2

Printed and bound in China by C&C Offset Printing Co. Ltd

To find out about all our publications, please visit **www.thamesandhudson.com**.
There you can subscribe to our e-newsletter, browse or download our current catalogue, and buy any titles that are in print.